The Christmas Book

Friendship

FAITH
ALIVE.
Christian Resources

GRAND RAPIDS, MICHIGAN

Acknowledgments

Faith Alive Resources is grateful to Geri Vooys for developing this resource book. A freelance author from Bloomingdale, New Jersey, Geri is music coordinator and organist at her church and director of the Friendship program, now in its twentieth year. Following completion of a degree program in music therapy, Geri served as a special education teacher; presently she teaches music for five nursery schools in her area.

The biblical backgrounds (Focusing on God's Word) for sessions 1 and 2 were adapted from those written for the first edition of the Friendship Bible Studies series by the late Harvey A. Smit, editor in chief of CRC Publications. Grace Pikaart, Assistant to the Director of Friendship Ministries, wrote the drama "Today, a Savior Is Born."

Special thanks to Nella Uitvlugt, Friendship Ministries Executive Director, for her valuable input and support, and to Diana Rock, Friendship consultant from Pittsburgh, Pennsylvania, for her critique of this book.

We're grateful to Friendship Ministries for paying the development costs of this book. Friendship Ministries is a nondenominational Christian foundation that promotes the spiritual development of youth and adults with intellectual disabilities and encourages churches to include these people in their fellowship. Thanks also to Ralph and Carol Honderd for their untiring efforts to raise funds for revision of the Friendship Bible Studies series and this resource book.

Illustrated by Jack Kershner, Kirby Huseby, Tim Foley, and Chris Schofield.

We welcome your comments. Call us at 1-800-333-8300 or e-mail us at editors@faithaliveresources.org or friendship@friendship.org. Or visit the Friendship website at www.Friendship.org.

ISBN 1-56212-903-1

10 9 8 7 6 5 4 3 2 1

Contents

Introduction

The mission of Friendship Ministries is to share God's love with people who have mental impairments and to enable them to become an active part of God's family. The Christmas season affords a wonderful opportunity for this to happen.

Friendship Bible Studies, a church education curriculum for youth and adults with mental impairments, forms the basis for Friendship Ministries. It is centered on Bible stories from both the Old and New Testament. This resource book is designed to complement the session plans found in the New Testament unit about Jesus' birth and to offer leaders a collection of ideas to use during a regular Christmas session or for special Christmas events.

LEADER TIP

The chart on the inside back cover of this guide presents an overview of Friendship Bible Studies and shows how this resource book and the Easter resource book enhance this curriculum. For additional information about organizing and leading a Friendship program, order the *Friendship Program Guide* (available from Faith Alive Christian Resources, 1-800-333-8300 or www.FaithAliveResources.org).

How Is This Resource Book Designed?

The materials for this book are grouped into two main categories:

- Session Plans
- Extras! Extras!

We'll explain each of these briefly on pages 5-6.

Session Plans

This resource book includes two session plans with directions for both the group meeting and one-on-one mentoring time. Like the session plans in the units for the Friendship Bible Studies series, they include the following six steps:

- Step 1: Greeting God and Each Other
- Step 2: Preparing to Listen to God's Story
- Step 3: Listening to God's Story
- Step 4: Reflecting on God's Story
- Step 5: Living into God's Story
- Step 6: Growing from God's Story

The first four steps in each of the two session plans are the responsibility of the group leader; the last two steps are covered by the one-on-one mentor.

LEADER TIP

Friendship groups who wish to continue their regular program routine during the Christmas season can simply incorporate the two session plans included in this book. You may want to use the second session plan ("The Wise Men's Visit") for an Epiphany celebration in January.

Some groups may want to vary their usual routine by adding or substituting some of the activities suggested in this resource book in place of the activities suggested in the regular session plans. (See description of Extras! Extras! below and options listed with each step in the session plans.)

Still other Friendship groups may wish to do something totally different for the Christmas season. This resource book offers worship ideas, dramas, and other activities to use as the focal point for special Christmas events.

Extras! Extras!

This section offers leaders and mentors a collection of ideas to incorporate into a regular Friendship Christmas session or to serve as the focal point for a special celebration. Included are

- directions for welcome activities.
- activities for praise and worship.
- dramas.
- directions for craft activities.
- ideas for service projects.
- ideas for celebrating Christmas and Epiphany.

Like the leader/mentor guides for the Friendship Bible studies, this resource book also includes

- words and music for the songs suggested in the session plans and throughout the book.
- directions for signing key words used in the session plans and throughout the book.
- patterns for story visuals, crafts, and so on.

Advent

Jesus left the comforts of heaven to bring us into the circle of God's family. What better time than Advent for your friends to experience what it means to be a part of God's family, especially within the faith community where they live and worship! May you see the love of Jesus in and through your friends as together you celebrate the birth of God's Son, our Savior.

That's our prayer for you! As God works through you and your friends, please let us know how this resource book has helped you. You can contact us with your comments and concerns at

Friendship Ministries
2850 Kalamazoo Ave. SE
Grand Rapids, MI 49560
1-800-333-8300
editors@faithaliveresources.org
friendship@friendship.org
www.Friendship.org

Our Savior Is Born

Scripture
Luke 2:1-20

Key Biblical Truth
God's promise to send a Savior came true when Jesus was born.

Group Session Goals
Friends and mentors will
- ☺ realize that Jesus is the One God promised to send to save us from our sins.
- ♡ thank God for sending Jesus to be our Savior.

Mentoring Session Goals
Friends and mentors
- ☺ review the story by completing at least one of the activities described in step 5.
- ☺ recite this memory verse:

  "Today in the town of David a Savior has been born to you. He is Christ the Lord."

  —Luke 2:11, NIrV

- ☺ read selected verses from the Christmas story in Luke 2:1-20.
- ♡ thank God for sending Jesus to be our Savior.
- 🖐 share the joy of Christmas with others in a tangible way.

Permission to photocopy this session plan for local Friendship program use is granted by CRC Publications.

Focusing on God's Word

Luke's exquisitely told narrative of Jesus' birth combines three elements: history, prophecy, and symbolism. It ends with the angels' joyful message to lowly shepherds who "gave glory and praise to God" (Luke 2:20).

History

The actual historical facts are related by Luke:

- A baby was born to Mary, a young girl who was engaged but not yet married.

- This baby was God's Son, conceived by the Holy Spirit (1:35).

- This baby was born in Bethlehem (according to the best calculations, during the year 4 B.C., probably not on December 25).

Prophecy

The prophetic element lies in the place of Christ's birth. Bethlehem was to be the origin of a new, great ruler of Israel who would come from the Lord and bring to his people greatness and peace (Micah 5:2-5). Jesus' birth fulfilled this prophecy.

Symbolism

The symbolic element lies in Luke's contrast between the birth of the King of kings and the fact that "there was no room for them in the inn" (Luke 2:7). That contrast runs though the rest of the story. The shepherds, the first witnesses to this great event, were common folk, despised because their occupation made them lax in religious observations.

The king was truly born in the most humble circumstances and received by the most humble among the Jewish people. The manger was the pivotal sign, since it was an unusual place for a baby; the angels told the shepherds to look for this unlikely setting as proof of the Savior's birth. This sign pointed to the way God would work through this newborn king—an unexpected, unusual way. God would bring salvation as promised, but not by military might or human power. Through human weakness, finally through one person's sacrificial death, God would bring new and better life to humankind.

> ## For All
>
> Likely your friends have experienced first-hand what it's like to be left out. Perhaps they've been excluded from a circle of friends, cheated out of appropriate education, denied work experience, ignored during worship—the list goes on. But not now, not at the manger, not at Christmas. The gift of Christmas is for *all*. The angels said,
>
> *"Do not be afraid. I bring you good news of great joy. It is for all the people."*
>
> —Luke 2:10
>
> Sing with great joy! Wrap your arms around your friends, and rejoice!

The most important point of this story is that the Son of God was born as a baby so that he might live among us. The Prince of heaven came to earth to become Immanuel, "God with us."

Good News of Great Joy

The first ones to celebrate Christmas with joyful song were an army of angels. The first to join from earth were the night-watching shepherds. Together they sang praises to God for the wonderful good news that they had told and heard—God's own Son had come to be the Savior of the world.

A band of shepherds were spending the night in the countryside near Bethlehem, caring for their sheep as usual. Then suddenly the glory of the Lord shone over the field. God's messenger, a great angel, appeared in that glory light and spoke to them. That light is a glorious sign of God's own presence.

The angel brought the message of redemption, turning the shepherds' fear into a joy that echoed the angels' song. For the message told them what God had done. It was God's "good news" that "today in the town of David a Savior has been born—Christ the Lord" (v. 11). That short sentence sums up the first gospel of Jesus Christ. Let this gospel message, the good news of salvation in Jesus, enter your hearts on the wings of joy.

LEADER TIP

You may prefer to end your first Christmas session with step 4, particularly if you will meet for more than one or two weeks in December. If you wish, save the mentoring session activities described on pages 15-18 for another session. Or plan a special session using activities described in the sections following session 2. You may want to save the story of the wise men (session 2) for January to celebrate Epiphany (see Celebration Ideas, pp. 97-98).

Suggested Songs

- "While Shepherds Watched" (p. 121)
- "Mary Had a Baby" (with signing, p. 111)
- "Emmanuel, Emmanuel" (with signing, p. 103)
- "Gloria/Glory" (with signing, p. 104)
- "Silent Night" (with dance directions, pp. 116-117)
- "O Come, All Ye Faithful" (chorus, p. 112)

A number of other songs are also included in the songs section of this book (see list on p. 99). If you wish, add or substitute some of these for those suggested in this session plan. You'll probably want music for other favorite carols your group likes to sing too.

Materials

- CD of favorite Christmas carols
- CD player
- Christmas reminders (see Leader Tip, p. 10)
- Sack or pillow case (optional)
- Large candle
- Small individual candles with drip guards or flashlights (optional)
- Bible (NIrV)
- Story visuals (photocopied from patterns on pp. 152-154)
- Markers or highlighters
- Flannel, felt, or flocked paper, glue, scissors
- Flannelboard
- Paper towel or toilet tissue tubes, shoe box, small gift box (optional)
- Photocopies or transparency of "Praise God, Jesus Is Born!" (p. 52)
- Supplies for optional activities (see boxes on pp. 10, 11, 14, 15)

STEP 1: Greeting God and Each Other

Welcome

As your friends arrive, have familiar Christmas carols playing in the background. Greet each person, and ask friend/mentor pairs to find one thing in the room that reminds them that it's Christmas time. Hint that you've hidden some things that are good to eat, some things to give away, and some for decorating our homes and Christmas trees. One reminds us of a gift that is for *everyone*.

LEADER TIP

Before your friends arrive, hide items around your room that remind us of Christmas: candy canes, stockings, ornaments, Christmas cards, candles, wrapped gifts, and so on. (If moving around is difficult for your friends, put the items in a sack or pillowcase. Have friends draw out one at a time.) You'll want one reminder for each friend/mentor pair. Make sure to hide a figure or picture of baby Jesus in the manger.

When all the reminders are found, stop the music and gather in your usual meeting place. Ask each pair, one at a time, to show their reminder, saving the pair who found the figure of Jesus for last. Ask each time, "Is this the most important part of Christmas?" When the figure of Jesus in the manger is shown, have everyone repeat the pair's answer: Yes! Affirm that Christmas is about Jesus—it's Jesus' birthday.

OPTIONAL WELCOME ACTIVITIES

Check out these ideas in the welcome activities section of this book:

- Christmas Maze (p. 31)
- Christmas Riddles (p. 32)
- Christmas Word/Picture Search (p. 33)
- Decorating the Christmas Tree (p. 34)
- More Tree Decorating Ideas (p. 35)

Some of the ideas suggested in the craft activities section (pp. 66-81) could also be used for welcome activities.

Praise and Worship

Many of your friends will have favorite Christmas carols that they love to sing. "While Shepherds Watched" (p. 121) is especially fitting with the Christmas story from Luke 2.

Teach your friends the African-American spiritual "Mary Had a Baby" and the signs for the phrase *"Baby, my Lord"* and *"Jesus"* (p. 111). You'll enjoy singing and signing the two short choruses "Emmanuel, Emmanuel"

(p. 103) and "Gloria/Glory" (p. 104). Note that this last chorus is also sung during step 3 as sound effects for the story.

Then sing "Silent Night" (p. 116) as you dim the lights and light a large candle. (You'll find directions for dance movements for "Silent Night" along with the music).

In this hushed mood, invite your group to prayer by singing the chorus of "O Come, All Ye Faithful" (p. 112). Join hands as you form a circle around the lighted candle. Lead the prayer time, or ask friends and mentors to offer sentence prayers of praise and thanksgiving. Conclude your prayer as you began—with the chorus of "O Come, All Ye Faithful."

OPTIONAL PRAISE AND WORSHIP ACTIVITIES

To vary or expand your praise and worship time, consider these ideas in the praise and worship section of this book:

- Advent Worship Plans: Good News (pp. 37-39)
- Advent Wreath: What Is Christmas? (p. 40)
- Celebrate Jesus' Birth! (responsive reading, p. 41)
- A Christmas Psalm (p. 42)
- Christmas Readings (selected poems, pp. 43-47)
- The Christmas Tree's Story (p. 48)

STEP 2: Preparing to Listen to God's Story

Open your Bible to Luke 2 and tell the group that today's Bible story tells about the gift God sent for us. Read Luke 2:11:

> *"Today in the town of David a Savior has been born to you. He is Christ the Lord."*

Encourage everyone in the group to say the verse together (see signing directions on pp. 123-124). Then talk about how long God's people had waited for a Savior to come. God had promised a Savior to Adam and Eve, and to Abraham and Isaac and Jacob, to Joseph, and to all God's people.

If you are using the Friendship Bible Studies series, and depending on where you are in the series (see list on inside back cover), you may want to spend some time reviewing the Old Testament stories and promises. Emphasize that God never forgot the promise that a Savior would be born. God did send a Savior! If you wish, use the responsive reading "Celebrate Jesus' Birth!" (p. 41) to emphasize this truth.

LEADER TIP

God's messengers had told about Jesus' birth for hundreds of years. The prophet Micah even told where Jesus would be born. Read Micah 5:2:

"Bethlehem, you might not be an important town in the nation of Judah, but out of you will come a ruler over Israel for me."

And finally it was time for Jesus to come. God had a surprise in store for some shepherds near Bethlehem—and a wonderful story of love for everyone!

STEP 3: Listening to God's Story

LEADER TIP

Ahead of time, photocopy the story visuals on pages 152-154 (Joseph, Mary, donkey, innkeeper, stable, cow, horse, baby Jesus, manger, shepherds, sheep, angels). You'll want several cows, horses, shepherds, sheep, and angels. Color with markers or highlighters. Glue a piece of flannel, felt, or flocked paper (available at craft supply stores) to each sheet of visuals; cut around each visual. (Or consider purchasing flannelgraph figures from church school supply catalogs or Christian bookstores.)

If you prefer to use the visuals as movable 3-D figures rather than with a flannelboard, attach each figure to a paper towel or toilet tissue tube cut to size. (If you want larger figures, enlarge them as you photocopy the patterns.) Glue the stable to a shoe box and the manger to a small gift box. Make sure everyone can see the diorama as the story unfolds.

Distribute the visuals to friend/mentor teams, and ask them to help you tell the story on cue. (If your group is large and you want everyone to have a visual, make additional angels, shepherds, and animals.)

Show your friends the flannelboard, and distribute the visuals you've prepared. Invite them to help you tell the story. If you wish to add sound effects to the story, divide your group into six teams and assign a mentor to coach each team. Whenever you say the words below, the assigned team will add the sound described in bold below and in the story. (If your group is small or if so much noise would be disruptive, omit some of the sounds.)

- donkey **("clip-clop")**
- crowds of people **(stamp feet, shout "Shalom")**
- knocked **(hit clenched fist again open palm)**
- animals **("moo," "neigh")**
- shepherds/sheep **("baa-baa")**
- angels **(sing "Gloria/Glory")**

Rehearse the sounds before you tell the story, and remind the group that you will call for the visuals and cue them when it's time to do the sound effects.

The story follows:

God's people had waited a long time for the promised Savior. Then one day the time came.

In those days, Caesar Augustus made a law. He wanted all the people he ruled to be counted in the town where their families first lived.

Joseph and Mary **(call for visuals)** set out for the little town of Bethlehem to be counted. Mary was expecting a baby. It was a long journey—walking and riding the donkey **(call for visual, cue for "clip-clop")**. Mary was tired. Joseph was tired. Even the donkey was tired! **(Cue for "clip-clop.")**

Finally they came to Bethlehem. There were crowds of people everywhere. **(Cue for stamping feet, "Shalom.")** It was almost dark. Joseph began to look for a place to spend the night.

Joseph knocked **(cue for knocking)** on every door up and down the street. Finally he knocked **(cue for knocking)** on the door of an inn at the end of the street. The innkeeper **(ask for visual)** said, "I'm sorry, I don't have a room for you."

Joseph looked at Mary. He could see that she was very tired. "But, sir, my wife is about to have a baby. We must have a place to stay."

The innkeeper looked at Mary. He could see she was very tired. "I do have a small stable in back. **(Ask for visual.)** You can stay there with the animals." **(Ask for visuals, cue for "moo," "neigh.")**

(Move Joseph and Mary visuals inside the stable.) Joseph made a bed of straw for Mary as the animals **(cue for "moo," "neigh")** watched. Mary lay down to sleep. The world was very still; the stars were shining bright.

Then something wonderful happened! In the quiet of the night, Mary's baby boy was born! **(Call for baby Jesus visual, place in Mary's arms.)** Mary laid him in a manger **(call for visual, move Jesus visual to manager)** filled with hay for the animals. **(Cue for "moo," "neigh.")** Joseph and Mary called the baby "Jesus." They knew that this baby was God's Son—the promised Savior! "Who would tell the good news?" Mary wondered. **(Pause to wonder.)**

Out in the fields near Bethlehem, shepherds were taking care of their sheep. **(Call for visual of shepherds and sheep, cue for "baa-baa.")** It was a quiet, chilly night.

Suddenly an angel **(call for visual)** stood by them and a bright light shone all around them. The shepherds were afraid; the sheep woke up, startled. **(Cue for "baa-baa.")**

The angel said, "Don't be afraid. I have good news for you and for all the world. Today a Savior is born in Bethlehem. You will find a baby wrapped in soft cloths and lying in a manger."

All at once the whole sky was filled with angels. **(Call for more angel visuals; cue for "Gloria/Glory.")**

Then the angels went back to heaven; all was quiet. **(Remove angels.)** The shepherds said to one another, "Let's go quickly to Bethlehem. Let's see what has happened."

The shepherds left their sheep **(cue for "baa-baa," move shepherds to the stable)** and hurried to Bethlehem. There they found Mary and Joseph and the baby, just as the angel had said. After they had seen Jesus, they told everyone what the angels said about this baby. They told everyone the good news that Jesus was the promised Savior!

OPTIONAL WAYS TO TELL THE STORY

Depending on your schedule, you might wish to combine praise and worship time with telling the Christmas story. We've included two ways to do that in the praise and worship section:

- ■ "The Gospel Message" (p. 49)
- ■ "The Nativity in Scripture and Song" (pp. 50-51)

If your group would enjoy a more dramatic presentation of the Christmas story, consider using one of the dramas from the drama section (pp. 53-65). You'll note that some are simple and short; others involve a larger cast of characters, costumes, and props. Some of the dramas are suitable for presentation. (You'll want to consider the range of ability in your group, the size of the group, and your schedule.)

STEP 4: Reflecting on God's Story

Ahead of time, make photocopies or a transparency of the prayer litany "Praise God, Jesus Is Born!" (p. 52). Then sing these songs again: "Mary Had a Baby" (p. 111), "Emmanuel, Emmanuel" (p. 103), and "Glory/Gloria" (p. 104). Add signing, and sing the last song in Spanish if you wish. End your group time with the prayer litany "Praise God, Jesus Is Born!" (p. 52).

OPTIONAL STEP 4 ACTIVITIES

Sing other favorite Christmas carols that reflect the story told in Luke 2:

- "Angels We Have Heard on High" (p. 101)
- "Away in a Manger" (p. 102)
- "Hark! the Herald Angels Sing" (p. 108)
- "Joy to the World" (p. 110)
- "O Little Town of Bethlehem" (p. 113)
- "Silent Night" (p. 116)

Or have one or more of your friends read one of the Christmas readings from the Praise and Worship section (pp. 36-52).

If you wish to involve your group in a craft activity, provide a large strip of mural paper (or roll ends of newsprint), markers, chalk, highlighters, paints and so on. Invite the group to illustrate the Bethlehem scene. Assign one team to draw the stable in the middle of the paper. Ask another team to draw the hillsides of Bethlehem off to one side of the paper and another to draw the town of Bethlehem on the opposite side of the paper. While these teams are working on the background scene, assign others to draw specific characters and animals. Provide construction paper, pencils, markers, and scissors, When the background is done, help glue the characters and animals in place. (If you want to move the shepherds from the fields to the stable, stick them on with poster putty. Use the same technique if you want to take the angels out of the scene.) Place your mural where others can enjoy it, and encourage friends to use it to retell the story.

For additional craft ideas, see the craft activities section, pages 66-81.

Mentoring Session for Youth or Adults

Materials for Youth and Adults

- Story visuals (photocopied from patterns on pp. 152-154)
- Scissors
- Crayons, colored pencils, markers, highlighters
- Paper punch
- Brightly colored yarn
- Clear tape
- Two 12" (30 cm) dowels or rulers
- Bible (NIrV) or picture Bible
- Christmas sticker (optional)
- Christmas card bookmark
- Small photo album (optional)

- Bright-colored cardstock, old Christmas cards, bits of ribbon, lace, beads, sequins, and so on
- Christmas card (photocopied from pattern on p. 136, optional)
- Supplies for optional activities (see boxes on pp. 17-18)

STEP 5: Living into God's Story

Review

Questions/Discussion Starters (Youth and Adult)
- Did God keep the promise to send a Savior?
- Was Jesus the One God promised?
- Name or point to the baby whom God sent.
- Name or point to Jesus' mother and Joseph.
- Name or point to the place where Jesus was born.
- Name or point to the animals that may have been in the stable.
- Name or point to those who sang about Jesus' birth.
- Name or point to the people who came to see Jesus.
- Tell who Jesus is. (God's Son, our Savior)
- Tell why Jesus came to earth. (to be our Savior, as God promised)
- Tell what the angels told the shepherds. (**Or sing "Gloria/Gloria."**)
- Show or tell how the shepherds felt when they heard the angels singing.
- Show or tell what the shepherds did after the angels told them about the baby Jesus.
- Tell Christmas story from Luke 2:1-20 in order. (**See optional review activities, p. 17.**)

Christmas Mobile (Youth and Adult)
Lay out the story visuals and invite your friend to color them with crayons, colored pencils, markers, or highlighters. (If you're short of time, color only the characters and omit the animals for the mobile.) Punch a hole in the top of each visual. Loop a length of yarn through the holes and tape in place.

Tape two dowels or rulers together to form an X. Wrap yarn around the middle to hold them in place. Tie the yarn attached to the visuals at various points along the mobile.

Mentor Helpline

When deciding how to review the Bible story, you will want to consider your friend's abilities. Ask simple questions first, then try the more difficult ones only if your friend is able to respond. Use the hand-over-hand technique to help with hands-on activities; recite the memory verse and read to your friend if he is not able to memorize or read. Adapt the activities to meet your friend's needs and life situation.

Mentor Helpline

You will need a photocopy of the story visuals (patterns on pp. 152-154) to use with the review questions and for making the mobile below. Copy the patterns on white cardstock and cut them out ahead of time. You may want to have your friend color the visuals before you ask the review questions.

To make a hanger, tie a loop of the yarn to the top of the mobile. The mobile will look something like the one shown here.

OPTIONAL REVIEW ACTIVITIES

If your friend is able to tell the events of the story in order, attach the story figures to craft sticks or paper towel tubing. Retell the story together using the visuals as puppets.

For a variety of other hands-on ideas, check the craft activities section (pp. 66-81). The following activities would be especially good for review:

- Modeling Clay Crèche (p. 77)
- "Stained Glass" Nativity Scene (pp. 79-80)

Recite (Youth and Adult)

We introduced the memory verse during the group session (see step 2, p. 11). Help your friend find Luke 2:11 in his Bible and read this verse together:

"Today in the town of David a Savior has been born to you. He is Christ the Lord."

Underline the verse with a highlighter or place a Christmas sticker in the margin. Then say the verse in phrases, repeating it several times together.

Read (Youth and Adult)

Have your friend find Luke 2 again, and insert a bookmark you've cut from an old Christmas card. Read the entire story together, or highlight and read verses 4-6, 8-11, 13-17. Ask your friend what his favorite part of the story is, and read those verses again.

Mentor Helpline

If memorizing is difficult for your friend, paraphrase the verse something like this: "Jesus has been born to you." If your friend is nonverbal, teach him to sign the memory verse (see pp. 123-124). If the task seems too difficult, sign only the words "a Savior has been born to you."

Mentor Helpline

If your friend has difficulty reading, bring a picture Bible. The *Read with Me Bible* (Zondervan Publishing House) uses minimal words and brightly colored pictures. Or make your own picture story from old Christmas cards and present this as a gift to your friend. (Cut the cards to size and slip then inside a small photo album.)

STEP 6: Growing from God's Story
(Youth and Adult)

Christmas is a time to share joy with others. Invite your friend to make Christmas cards for family and friends and others in your faith community.

Provide half sheets of bright-colored cardstock folded in half, old greeting cards, glue, bits of lace, beads, and so on, and show your friend how to use these materials to decorate the old front of the folded cards. (If you wish, photocopy the card pattern on p. 136. You may want to cut scenes and other interesting pieces from the old cards ahead of time if this is difficult for your friends.)

Help your friend write a simple greeting inside the card and sign his name. Suggest that he hand-deliver or mail the card to the special person.

OPTIONAL STEP 6 ACTIVITIES

If your friends enjoy making cards, you might want to make this a group activity. We've described ways for making Christmas cards as a service project or fund-raiser in the service project section (see p. 84).

The service project section offers several other options for serving at home and church and for reaching out into the community to bring cheer to those who are shut in or in need. Many of the crafts described in the craft activities section (pp. 66-81) can be made as gifts for family and friends or used as decorations for special gatherings with family and friends.

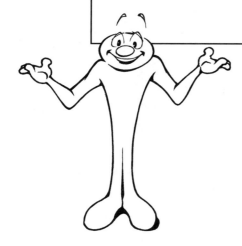

The Wise Men's Visit

Scripture
Matthew 2:1-12

Key Biblical Truth
Like the wise men, we praise and honor Jesus because Jesus is God's Son.

Group Session Goals
Friends and mentors will

☺ realize that Jesus deserves their love and praise.

♡ participate in an act of praise to Jesus, God's Son, our Savior.

Mentoring Session Goals
Friends and mentors will

☺ review the story by completing at least one of the activities described in Step 5.

☺ recite this memory verse:

"Today in the town of David a Savior has been born to you. He is Christ the Lord."

—Luke 2:11, NIrV

☺ read selected verses from story of the wise men in Matthew 2:1-12.

♡ praise Jesus, God's Son, our Savior.

🌳 share the good news about Jesus in one specific way.

Permission to photocopy this session plan for local Friendship program use is granted by CRC Publications.

Focusing on God's Word

The nativity scenes displayed in store windows or in our homes typically include the baby Jesus, Mary, Joseph, shepherds, and wise men. But reading between the lines of Matthew's account, we can conclude that the wise men probably weren't there.

The star appeared in the sky either at the time of Jesus' conception or at his birth. After sighting the star, the wise men made preparations for a long journey and began their travel. As much as a year may have passed before they reached the land of Israel.

King of Kings!

Psalm 72 calls Jesus God's "royal son" (v. 1). Somehow, despite the circumstances, the shepherds caught a glimpse of this at the manger. The wise men, entwined in their pagan beliefs, followed a star they were sure was telling of a new king. They worshiped with so little convincing. Yet we, with all of God's revelation in the written Word, sometimes miss the grandeur of the gift—a King born for each one of us. Because of this very King who was willing to die on the cross, we are all royal sons and daughters.

O come, worship the King! *"And he shall reign, King of kings, and Lord of lords . . . forever and ever."* Let these words and the beautiful music from Handel's *Messiah* ring in your heart and mind this season.

We find Herod ordering his solders to kill all the boys in Bethlehem of two years and under (Matt. 2:16), a directive based on his careful checking with the wise men as to when the star first appeared in the sky (2:7). Besides, when the travelers from the east finally arrived in Bethlehem, we're told they found the baby Jesus and his parents living in a house (2:11)—likely this was some time later.

Matthew is the only gospel writer who tells the story of the wise men. Their coming is significant in that they were the first Gentiles to pay homage to the King of the Jews. They were the first of the flood of converts who would follow, the beginning of the fulfillment of Psalm 72:8-11.

These wise men were actually *magi* or astrologers. They practiced the ancient pagan art of seeking knowledge of earthly events by studying the configuration of the planets and movement of the stars. You need not explain their actual character, but be careful not to imply that they were smart men worthy of special recognition.

Songwriters and storytellers often speak of these wise men as "three kings from the Orient" and name them Melchior, Caspar, and Balthasar. But the Bible doesn't call them kings, give them names, or tell their number. The idea of *three* wise men comes from the three gifts they gave: gold, incense, and myrrh (v. 11). These were precious gifts fit for a king.

The star that appeared in the sky was a sign given to these men of the East that the Messiah was born. Like the sign to the shepherds (the babe in the manger), this was something unusual enough to testify to a special happening. The star was designed to fit the magi's belief that this light in the sky indicated a new king, someone to whom people of other lands should also pay homage. So the wise men came to Israel, seeking the new king.

They found ignorance and indifference. The people of Israel seemed not to have noticed the star, nor made inquiry about its meaning. When the wise men asked about it in Jerusalem, they alerted King Herod to a possible threat to his power. The scribes were able to give them the desired information—the Messiah would be born in Bethlehem (Micah 5:2). The wise men proceeded there, joyfully paid homage to the young King, and, warned by God in a dream, went back to their own land without stopping as promised in Jerusalem.

The wise men worshiped the Son of God! Even though they might not have realized it, this baby was indeed God in human form, God's own Son with us. The wise men knelt before him; they honored him and praised him. Today we still bow before this infant King. We sing songs and bring him gifts of love and praise. We praise Jesus, God's gift of salvation to us.

Suggested Songs

- "Mary Had a Baby" (with signing, p. 111)
- "Emmanuel, Emmanuel" (with signing, p. 103)
- "We Three Kings" (stanza 1 and chorus with dance movements, pp. 118-119)
- "O Come, All Ye Faithful" (chorus, p. 112)
- "Gloria, Glory" (p. 104)
- "He Came Down" (p. 109)

Materials

- Black or navy mural paper or posterboard or navy sheet
- Stars (photocopied from pattern on p. 149)
- Yellow cardstock for stars
- Glue and glitter, small star stickers, tinsel, gold and silver garland
- Poster putty or double-faced tape, stapler
- Three gifts (see Leader Tip, p. 23)
- Star headbands (see Leader Tip, p. 24)
- Simple costumes (optional—see Leader Tip, pp. 24 and 25)
- Supplies for optional activities
- Supplies for optional activities (see boxes on pp. 22, 23, 25, 26)

STEP 1 : Greeting God and Each Other

Welcome

Set the stage for this session by creating a star-filled mural. Lay out stars, scissors, glue sticks and glitter, small star stickers, tinsel, bits of silver and gold garland. Invite friends and mentors to decorate stars and stick them on the navy background with poster putty or double-faced tape.

As some finish, ask them to help you staple silver and gold garland around the edge of the large star. Place this in the center of your mural, pointing out that this star reminds you of the one the wise men followed to find Jesus, the newborn King.

OPTIONAL WELCOME ACTIVITIES

If you're planning an Epiphany celebration, you might want friends and mentors to make stars to decorate your room and crowns to wear (see "Welcome Back Party," p. 98). This would also be a good time to collect gifts for the needy if you plan to make that a part of your Epiphany celebration (see p. 97).

The craft activities section offers the following ideas for decorating for a party:

- Christmas Stars (p. 73)
- Foil Star Ornaments (p. 74)
- Stamp Art Place Mats (p. 81)

To emphasize the star theme, provide various sizes of flashlights (penlight, regular flashlight, heavy-duty flashlight, and emergency lantern). Depending on how many flashlights you have, choose a group of friends to operate them. Turn off the lights and have the friends shine their lights around on the ceiling. Emphasize that the lantern-size light is like the bright star that the wise men followed. Give each friend a turn shining one of the lights.

Praise and Worship

To review the Christmas story, sing "Mary Had a Baby" (p. 111). Especially emphasize the third stanza, *"She named him King Jesus . . ."* and sign *"King Jesus."* Sing the chorus "Emmanuel, Emmanuel" (p. 103) and sign *"God with us."* To introduce today's story, sing the first stanza and chorus (or just the chorus) of "We Three Kings."

If you did this last time, dim the room lights and light a large candle to invite your group to prayer. Sing the chorus of "O Come, All Ye Faithful" (p. 112) and join hands in a circle around the lighted candle. Lead the prayer time, or ask friends and mentors to offer sentence prayers of praise and thanksgiving. Conclude your prayer with the chorus of "O Come, All Ye Faithful."

STEP 2: Preparing to Listen to God's Story

LEADER TIP

Ahead of time, prepare three gifts to represent the gifts the wise men brought. Place some gold foil-wrapped coins in a clear container; add a shiny gold bow to the lid. Add a ribbon to a fancy clear glass bottle of perfume. Place a mixture of spices (cinnamon sticks, whole cloves, fruit-flavored tea bags, orange peel, and so on) in a small wooden box. Make sure all the containers can be opened easily.

Open your Bible to Luke 2:11, and invite your group to join you in telling the good news of Christmas:

"Today in the town of David a Savior has been born to you. He is Christ the Lord."

Repeat the verse again, making sure everyone is participating in some way (for signing directions, see pp. 123-124). Emphasize how excited the shepherds were to find the baby in the manger, just as the angels had told them, and how the shepherds worshiped this baby. Wonder who else would come to see this wonderful gift from God. How would they know that Jesus had come?

Hint that a star (point to your mural or hold up a star) and three gifts (pass around the three gifts you've prepared) are part of the story you'll tell today. Encourage your friends to look, smell, and feel the gifts. Wonder if they would be fit to give to a king. Wonder what you and everyone in your group could bring to a king.

STEP 3: Listening to God's Story

LEADER TIP Narrate the story yourself, and ask five mentors or friends who are good readers to play the parts of the five stars. (Or have friend/mentor teams read and pantomime the parts together.) Ahead of time, make a star headband for each actor from the pattern on page 148. (Photocopy four patterns on yellow cardstock as shown; enlarge the fifth star 100 percent as you copy. Staple the extension piece to the stars, adjusting them to fit the actors. Make two sets if you're using friend/mentor teams.) If you wish, supply large yellow T-shirts or bath towels tied at the waist with gold Christmas garland. Use the star mural the group created as a backdrop for the stage area.

Introduce the "stars" who will tell the story. Explain that stars really can't talk, but you want everyone to imagine what they might have said if they could have talked when Jesus was born. Listen closely. . . .

The story follows:

Narrator: On that night in Bethlehem so long ago, angels sang, "Glory to God in the highest, peace to you on earth." The excited shepherds hurried to Bethlehem and worshiped the baby in the manger. Mary watched and wondered what all this meant—her baby, God's Son, was the Savior of the world! "The shepherds heard the good news from the angels, but who will tell the others all around the world?" Mary asked herself. The stars shone brightly as Mary wondered about all that had happened.

First Star: Maybe you've seen me up in the sky. I like to twinkle with all the millions of stars in the sky. Most of you look up and know that God created stars and hung them in the sky. For many years, people have studied the stars and wondered about the God who made them. What excitement there must have been that night when a new star appeared! Wise men who lived far away from Bethlehem saw the big, bright star in the East **(point to big star)**.

Second Star: I watched as the wise men looked up into the sky. One of them said, "Look, a new star! Do you know what it means?" Then I heard another one answer, "It means a child has been born somewhere. Surely this big beautiful star means that a king has been born! Let's follow the star and find the new king!"

Narrator: So the wise men began their search for the new king. They prepared their camels for a long journey and packed beautiful gifts: precious gold, expensive perfume, and sweet-smelling spices. **(Display gifts used in step 2.)**

Big Star: It was strange to see the wise men looking up at me. I was the biggest, brightest star they had ever seen. Night after night, the wise men followed me through strange lands where they had never been before. On and on they traveled, until they reached the great city of Jerusalem.

Everywhere they went they asked people, "Where is the King of the Jews? We have seen his star in the East and have come to worship him." None of the people knew anything about this King. How amazing! They had not heard the good news!

Third Star: The wise men made a visit to King Herod, who lived in the palace in Jerusalem. When he heard that wise men were looking for a new king, he was alarmed. He wanted to be the only king! King Herod called the teachers of the law and asked, "Where is the Christ to be born?" The teachers, said, "In the little town of Bethlehem."

Narrator: King Herod called for the wise men and pretended to be friendly. "I will help you," he said. "Go to Bethlehem and look there for the new king. When you have found him, come and tell me, for I also want to worship him." (King Herod was trying to trick the wise men. He really wanted to hurt the newborn king.)

Fourth Star: The wise men followed the big star **(point to big star)** to Bethlehem. The big star stopped right over a little house in Bethlehem. There they saw Mary and the child Jesus. He looked like any other little boy, but the wise men knew he was no ordinary child. This was the young King for whom they had looked for such a long time! "O King Jesus," they said, "how glad we are to have found you!" They worshiped him. They brought their gifts—gold, perfume, and spices—and laid them before him **(show gifts you used in step 2).**

Narrator: God warned the wise men in a dream not to go back to King Herod. So they went back home to their own country a different way. Their hearts were happy—they had found the new King, Jesus, God's Son.

OPTIONAL WAYS TO TELL THE STORY

If you wish to involve the larger group, invite them to sing some of these songs:

- "Gloria/Glory" (p. 104) just as the story begins.
- "We Three Kings" (pp. 118-119) just before the big star speaks.
- "O Little Town of Bethlehem" (p. 113) following the teacher's answer to King Herod.
- "O Come, All Ye Faithful" (p. 112) as the narrator concludes the story.

Or try these variations:

- *First-person Accounts.* The entire story could be told in the first person from the point of the view of the one big star or from the experience of one of the wise men. Choose someone who has a flair for dramatic storytelling. This is especially effective if your group is small. You'll want to provide a copy of the rewritten script and a simple costume for the actor.
- *Pantomime.* Add the three wise men, King Herod, Mary, and the young child Jesus to the cast. (Either use a large doll or invite a mother and her one-year-old child to play the part of Mary and Jesus.) Have your friends wear simple costumes and pantomime the actions of the story. (You'll want to rewrite the script a bit, adding specific actions throughout.)

STEP 4: Reflecting on God's Story

Focus the group's attention on the acts of worship found in both the Christmas story from Luke 2 and the story from Matthew 2. Highlight these verses in your Bible and accent the action words as you read:

> *[The shepherds] hurried off and found Mary and Joseph and the baby. . . . After the shepherds had seen him, they told everyone. . . . The shepherds . . . gave glory and praise to God.* (Luke 2:16-18, 20)
>
> *Wise Men from the east came . . . to worship him. . . . When they saw the star, they were filled with joy. . . . They saw the child. . . . They bowed down and worshiped him. . . . They gave him gold, incense and myrrh.* (Matthew 2:1-2, 10-11)

Point out that the shepherds and the wise men used their hands and feet and their whole bodies to come to worship Jesus. They used their voices to tell others the good news. And they used their hearts filled with joy to praise God. Explain that worship is the best gift we can bring to Jesus, and invite your friends to do that right now.

Sing the song "Gloria/Glory" (p. 104). When the group sings, "*Glory, glory, glory be to God on high,*" lift hands in praise. Sing "He Came Down" and sign the words *hope, peace, love, joy* (p. 125).

OPTIONAL STEP 5 ACTIVITIES

To vary or extend this closing worship, you may wish to sing additional songs:

■ "Good News" (p. 105)
■ "Emmanuel, Emmanuel" (p. 103)
■ "Go, Tell It on the Mountain" (p. 107)

Or, if you haven't already used them, invite friends or mentors to share one or both of these readings:

■ Wise Men Worship (p. 49)
■ "Thank You, God" (p. 46)

After the reading, invite friend/mentor pairs to finish this sentence as their own prayer: *"Thank you God, for . . ."* Or have volunteers portray still-life scenes as described on page 46.

Materials for Youth and Adults

- Story cards (photocopied from patterns on pp. 150-151)
- White cardstock for story cards and poems
- Crayons, colored pencils, markers, highlighters
- Paper punch, length of heavy yarn
- Small photo album (optional)
- Bible (NIrV)
- Wise men sticker (optional)
- Christmas card bookmark
- Pliable craft or florist wire
- Red and white (or gold) beads
- Poems (photocopied from readings on pp. 43 and 47)
- Narrow red or white ribbon
- Supplies for optional activity (see box on p. 29)

STEP 5: Living into God's Story

Review

You will need a photocopy of the story cards (patterns on pp. 150-151) to use with the review questions below and for making the banner described on page 28. Copy the cards on white cardstock and cut them apart ahead of time. You may want to have your friend color the cards before you ask the review questions.

Questions/Discussion Starters (Youth and Adult)

Lay the story cards out in order in front of your friend. Use the following questions (listed in order of increasing difficulty) to guide your review.

- Did the wise men try to find Jesus?
- Did the star point them to Jesus?
- Did the wise men worship (praise and honor) Jesus?
- Name or point to the ones who came to worship Jesus.
- Name or point to the one the wise men were looking for.
- Point to the star that showed the wise men where to go.
- Tell who Jesus is. (God's Son, our Savior)
- Tell how the wise men praised and honored Jesus.
- List some ways we can praise and honor Jesus.
- Tell the story of the wise men's visit in order (**See story card banner activity on page 28.**)

> ## Mentor Helpline
>
> If your friend is unable to tell the story in order, number the cards in order. If your friend is able to tell the events of the story in order, mix up the cards before stringing them together. Have your friend decide which card should be first, and so on. Remember to string the cards from left to right in the order they would be "read," using the hand-over-hand technique as needed.

Story Card Banner (Youth and Adult)

Lay out the story cards, and invite your friend to color them with crayons, colored pencils, markers, or highlighters. Punch a hole in the upper left and right corners of each story card. (See Mentor Helpline on p. 27.) Help your friend string a length of yarn through the holes so that the yarn is on the back side of one card; repeat with each card until you've made a banner of cards. Knot each end of the yarn, forming loops to hang the banner.

Recite (Youth and Adult)

We reviewed the memory verse during the group session (see step 2, p. 23). Help your friend find Luke 2:11 in her Bible and read this verse together. (If you haven't already done so, mark the verse with a sticker showing the wise men or with a bookmark cut from a recycled Christmas card with a picture of the wise men.)

Say the verse in phrases several times; then say the entire verse again. Add signing for some or all of the words, if you wish (pp. 123-124).

Read (Youth and Adult)

Help your friend find Matthew 2 in her Bible, and insert a bookmark cut from a recycled Christmas card with a picture of the wise men. Read the entire story (vv. 1-12) together, or highlight and read verses 1-3, 7-11.

Ask your friend what her favorite part of the story was. Have her imagine that she was one of the wise men. Would she have been scared of King Herod? What would have been the most exciting part? How would she have worshiped King Jesus? (For instance, sing a song, give Jesus a kiss, kneel down and give God thanks, and so on). Emphasize that your friend doesn't have to be one of the wise men to worship Jesus.

Mentor Helpline

If your friend is a nonreader, use a picture Bible again to share the story. Or simply use the story cards to "read" the story together. Ask your friend to show or tell how each scene makes her feel. (If you made a photo album Bible last time you might prefer to add the story cards to the album rather than making the banner described above. See Mentor Helpline, p. 17.)

STEP 6: Growing from God's Story (Youth and Adult)

Ahead of time, copy one or both of these poems on cardstock:

- ■ God's Gift (p. 43)
- ■ Wise Men Worship (p. 47)

Cut out the poems to make small cards; punch a hole in the corner of each card. You'll also want to purchase pliable craft or floral wire and red beads from a craft store for the heart and white (or gold) beads for the star ornaments. Cut the wire into 10" (25 cm) lengths for the hearts and 12" (30 cm) lengths for the star. Twist a tiny loop on one end.

Invite your friends to make simple ornament gifts to tell others the good news about Jesus. String the beads on a length of wire, slipping the beads toward the looped end. When the wire is full of beads, twist another tiny loop on the end.

Bend the beaded wires into heart or star shapes as shown below. With narrow red or white ribbon, attach the "God's Gift" cards to the hearts and "Wise Men Worship" cards to the stars. Give the gifts as tray favors to a nursing home or assisted living center in your community.

OPTIONAL STEP 6 ACTIVITIES

You might want to combine the ornament activity with caroling to elderly people in your church and community. This and several other opportunities for your group to bring the good news to others are described in the service projects section (pp. 82-92).

Welcome Activities

- ■ Christmas Maze
- ■ Christmas Riddles
- ■ Christmas Word/Picture Search
- ■ Decorating the Christmas Tree
- ■ More Tree Decorating Ideas

LEADER TIP

These activities are appropriate ones to have set up as your group members arrive. But you could also use them later in a session to introduce the story or as a response to the story. Or they could serve as an activity for a party or family night. Be sure to check out the craft activities section for other ideas you could use to welcome your friends.

Unless otherwise indicated, permission to photocopy materials in this section for local Friendship program use is granted by CRC Publications.

LEADER TIP

This activity can be photocopied and used as is by individual friend/mentor teams. For a more action-filled activity, set up a maze in your room and invite friends and mentors to follow the path to the manger. Have a life-size manger with a baby doll set up at the end of the path. (You'll want to make sure your maze is accessible to people with limited mobility and to those in wheelchairs.)

Can You Find Baby Jesus?

The angels told the shepherds in the fields to go to Bethlehem. They would find a baby wrapped in cloths and lying in a manger. Help the shepherds find the path to the manager.

LEADER TIP   Use these riddles alone or in combination with the ornament patterns on pages 137-140 in the back of this book (see also tree decorating activity on p. 34).

I'm shaped like a shepherd's staff. I'm red and white. I'm good to eat. What am I?

I shine in the sky at night. I guided the wise men to Bethlehem. What am I?

I'm too big to wear on your foot. I like to be hung up and filled with small gifts. What am I?

God chose me to be the mother of baby Jesus. Who am I?

I am green and prickly. I like to be decorated for Christmas. What am I?

I went with Mary to Bethlehem to be counted. There was no room for us in the inn. Who am I?

I'm round and pretty, but I break easily. I can be hung on your Christmas tree. What am I?

I was born in a manger. I am God's Son, your Savior. Who am I?

I come in many sizes. I can be lit. I remind you that Jesus is the light of the world. What am I?

We were taking care of our sheep the night Jesus was born. We went to Bethlehem to worship him. Who are we?

I make a jingle, jingle sound. I ring out the story of Christmas. What am I?

This is what we told the shepherds the night Jesus was born: "Glory to God in the highest, and on earth peace, goodwill to men." Who are we?

I am made of wood. Jesus was laid in one when he was born. What am I?

We followed a star to Bethlehem. We brought gifts to Jesus. Who are we?

Christmas Word/Picture Search

Below are words/pictures from the Christmas story. Search across and down to find each word/picture.

- Angels
- Bethlehem
- Donkey
- Gifts
- Jesus
- Joseph

- Manger
- Mary
- Sheep
- Shepherds
- Star
- Wise Men

If you wish to use this as a group game, photocopy the game, enlarging it 200 percent, and mount on posterboard. Copy the word/picture cards (patterns on pp. 155-158) on bright-colored cardstock. Hide these cards throughout your room, and invite friend/mentor teams to find one card, match it to the word/picture on the game board, and draw a circle around the word/picture. (If you have more than twelve teams in your group, make two game boards and two sets of cards. If you have fewer teams, encourage teams to find additional cards.)

LEADER TIP

Decorating a tree is a fun way to begin your first Christmas session. Try one or more of the ideas below.

LEADER TIP You may be able to purchase an artificial tree for a minimal amount from a consignment shop or perhaps advertise in your church bulletin or newsletter for a used tree. We suggest that you string the lights on the tree before your session begins.

Use the patterns on pages 137-140 in the back of this book to make ornaments for your tree. Copy the patterns on bright-colored cardstock and cut them out if this is difficult for your friends. (You'll want one or more ornaments for each person in your group.) Provide glue sticks, bits of old greeting cards, ribbon, glitter, and so on for them to decorate the ornaments. Punch out the hole, and slip a paper clip or ornament hanger through the hole. If you wish, combine this activity with the Christmas riddles on p. 32 or with "The Christmas Tree's Story," a praise and worship activity described on p. 48.

Invite each friend and mentor to bring one ornament to place on the tree. So that you can identify the owners later, cut small tags from index cards, punch a hole in each, and tie a nametag to each ornament with string or Christmas ribbon.

Give each friend and mentor a small note-sized piece of bright-colored cardstock. Invite them to write one thing that makes them happy and joyful this Christmas (or draw a picture, if writing is difficult). Punch a hole at the top of the note and tie a length of narrow red or green ribbon through it to make a loop. Hang the "joy notes" on the tree and sing "Joy to the World" (p. 110).

Collect 1" (2.5 cm) Styrofoam balls, long corsage pins, and sequins and beads of various sizes and colors. (Beads from old jewelry work well.) Show your friends how to thread a corsage pin first with a large sequin, then with two or three beads, and ending with a smaller sequin. (You'll want to leave about 1/2" of the pin showing.) Dab glue on the end of the pin and insert it into the ball. Fill at least three more pins with sequins and beads; glue them evenly around the ball. Attach a ribbon loop hanger to a regular straight pin, dab with glue, and insert into the ball.

Provide satin Christmas balls and invite friends to decorate them with glitter glue. They can make designs, write their names on the ball, and so on. To make a hanger, glue narrow ribbon around the ball, leaving a loop at the top.

You'll need a collection of old Christmas cards and plastic lids from yogurt, Pringles, and so on. Cut circular pictures from the Christmas cards, making them slightly smaller than the plastic lids. Provide glue sticks for friends to glue a picture on each side of the plastic lid. (Or if you prefer, cut circles of red or green felt for the back side of each lid.) Use a large needle to poke two holes in the rim of each lid; thread yarn or narrow ribbon through the two holes and knot above to make a hanger.

Bake and decorate Christmas cookies to hang on the tree. This recipe is pliable enough to take any form and still hold its shape during baking.

1 cup butter or margarine

1 cup firmly packed brown sugar

4 eggs

1/2 cup light or dark molasses

8-10 cups unsifted flour

2 tsp. baking soda

1 tsp. salt

1 tsp. ginger

2 tsp. cinnamon

Cream butter with brown sugar. Beat in eggs one at a time. Stir in molasses. Add 2 cups of the flour, baking soda, salt, spices. Gradually stir in the remaining flour until the dough is stiff and pliable like clay. Wrap dough; chill two hours.

Roll dough on floured surface to 1/4-inch thickness. Dip various shaped cookie cutters in flour and cut out cookies. Place on lightly greased cookie sheets. Mark designs on cookies using toothpicks, forks, and glasses. Sprinkle with colored sugar. (Or if you prefer, bake, frost the cookies, and decorate with colored sugar.) Cut a paper straw into 1/2-inch lengths; poke a section of straw through the top of each cookie. Bake at 350 degrees for 12-15 minutes. While the cookie is warm, pull the straw out; cool. Insert narrow colored ribbon into the hole, and hang the cookies on the tree.

Praise & Worship Activities

- Advent Worship Plans: Good News
- Advent Wreath: What Is Christmas?
- Celebrate Jesus' Birth!
- A Christmas Psalm
- Christmas Readings
  - A Christmas Prayer
  - God's Gift
  - Jesus Is Born
  - One Starry Night
  - "Thank You, God"
  - Wise Men Worship
- The Christmas Tree's Story
- The Gospel Message
- The Nativity in Scripture and Song
- Praise God, Jesus Is Born! (Litany)

LEADER TIP The activities included in this section can be used as optional praise and worship activities during your regular session. They can also be used for family night gatherings and Christmas programs or for worship with your larger church family. Look for opportunities to place your friends in leadership roles in any of these settings.

 Unless otherwise indicated, permission to photocopy materials in this section for local Friendship program use is granted by CRC Publications.

LEADER TIP

We've included a series of simple worship plans for the season of Advent. The plans focus around lighting the candles of the Advent wreath. (Directions for making the wreath are included on pp. 69 in the craft activities section.)

You can use these plans for your praise and worship time during your regular Friendship sessions. (Music for the suggested songs is included on pp. 99-121 in the songs section.) If your group only meets for two weeks during December, combine two weeks into one and omit some of the Scripture readings and songs if necessary. You'll note that we've included the lighting of the Christ candle as part of week four.

Also consider sharing these service plans with your church worship committee. They can be adapted to the larger service and offer a way to involve your friends in corporate worship. Suggest that all or many of the suggested songs be included and that your friends be involved in lighting the candles. (You'll want to save the lighting of the Christ candle for Christmas Day.) Ask that the Scripture be read from the New International Reader's Version (NIrV) as included in the plans here.

First Week of Advent

Song: "Good News"

Scripture: Lamentations 3:25-26

The LORD is good to those who put their hope in him. He is good to those who look to him. It is good when people wait quietly for the LORD to save them.

Leader: God's people waited a long, long time, hoping for the promised Savior to come. We light the candle of hope to remind us that their hope was turned to joy when Jesus was born in Bethlehem.

Lighting the Candle of Hope: Jesus came down that we may have hope.

Songs: "O Little Town of Bethlehem" (stanza 1)
"He Came Down" *(that we may have hope)*
"Good News"

Second Week of Advent

Song: "Good News"

Scripture: Isaiah 9:6-7

A child will be born to us. A son will be given to us. He will rule over us. And he will be called Wonderful Adviser and Mighty God. He will also be called Father Who Lives Forever and Prince Who Brings Peace. . . . The peace he brings will never end.

Leader: We are all sinners. That makes us enemies of God. But because God loved us and sent Jesus, his Son, to be our Savior, we can have peace with God. We light the candle of peace to remind us that we can have peace with God forever in heaven.

Lighting the Candle of Hope: Jesus came down that we may have hope.

Lighting the Candle of Peace: Jesus came down that we may have peace.

Songs: "Hark the Herald Angels Sing" (stanza 1)
"He Came Down" *(that we may have hope . . . peace)*
"Good News"

Third Week of Advent

Song: "Good News"

Scripture: John 3:16

God loved the world so much that he gave his one and only Son. Anyone who believes in him will not die but will have eternal life.

Leader: Christmas is a time for gifts. God gave the greatest gift of all—Jesus, his own Son. We light the candle of love to remind us of God's love for us in sending Jesus to be our Savior.

Lighting the Candle of Hope: Jesus came down that we may have hope.

Lighting the Candle of Peace: Jesus came down that we may have peace.

Lighting the Candle of Love: Jesus came down that we may have love.

Songs: "Ring the Bells"
"He Came Down" *(that we may have hope . . . peace . . . love)*
"Good News"

LEADER TIP

If "Ring the Bells" isn't familiar to your group, invite your friends to sing *"Ring the bells"* each time and ring small jingle bells pinned to a wristband of grosgrain ribbon. Have mentors sing the rest of the words as a response.

Fourth Week of Advent

Song: "Good News"

Scripture: Luke 2:10-11

"I bring you good news of great joy. It is for all the people. Today in the town of David a Savior has been born to you. He is Christ the Lord."

Leader: The shepherds in the fields were the first to hear the good news that Jesus had come. This good news is for all people—for you and for me!

We light the candle of joy to praise God for Jesus, the baby born in Bethlehem, who is our Savior.

Lighting the Candle of Hope: Jesus came down that we may have hope.

Lighting the Candle of Peace: Jesus came down that we may have peace.

Lighting the Candle of Love: Jesus came down that we may have love.

Lighting the Candle of Joy: Jesus came down that we may have joy.

Songs: "Joy to the World" (stanza 1)
"He Came Down" *(that we may have hope . . . peace . . . love . . . joy)*

Scripture: Luke 1:31-33

[The angel said to Mary,] "You must name him Jesus. He will be great and will be called the Son of the Most High God. The Lord God will make him a king. . . . He will rule forever over his people. . . . His kingdom will never end."

Leader: Jesus came as a baby in Bethlehem. He died on the cross to save us from our sins. Now Jesus is in heaven, and he will come again to take us to be with him forever. We light the Christ candle to celebrate the birthday of Jesus, our King!

Lighting of the Christ Candle: Jesus came that we may have life.

Songs: "He Came Down" *(that we may have hope . . . peace . . . love . . . joy . . . life)*
"Good News"

LEADER TIP

This is a way to incorporate the Advent wreath into one session or a special celebration. (We've included directions for making a wreath on p. 69.) Divide the group into two speaking groups; select one or more people from group two—possibly some who are nonverbal—to light the five candles. Note that the Scripture passages are familiar Christmas verses, probably ones your group already knows. (We've taken them from the New International Reader's Version; you'll want to select the version that is the most familiar to your friends.) If your friends are readers, make photocopies or a transparency of this reading.

Group 1: A child will be born to us. A son will be given to us. (Isaiah. 9:6)

Group 2: We light this candle for the hope of Christmas.

Group 1: "May glory be given to God in the highest heaven! And may peace be given to those he is pleased with on earth!" (Luke 2:14)

Group 2: We light this candle for the peace of Christmas.

Group 1: God loved the world so much that he gave his one and only Son. (John 3:16)

Group 2: We light this candle for the love of Christmas.

Group 1: "I bring you good news of great joy. It is for all the people. Today in the town of David a Savior has been born to you." (Luke 2:10-11)

Group 2: We light this candle for the joy of Christmas.

Group 1: Anyone who believes in him will not die but will have eternal life. (John 3:16)

Group 2: We light this candle for the Christ of Christmas.

Reader: The prophets came to Israel to tell them what to do. They pointed to the birth of Christ, and what they said came true.

All: Rejoice and celebrate! Jesus, our King, has come!

Reader: In Bethlehem in a cattle stall a miracle we find: that such a lowly place should hold the Savior of mankind!

All: Rejoice and celebrate! Jesus, our Savior, has come!

Reader: The shepherds watched their flocks of sheep when light broke from the sky. They heard a dazzling angel say, "A child is born nearby."

All: Rejoice and celebrate! Jesus, our Savior, has come!

Reader: The angels sang a midnight song, their eyes were filled with joy: "The Son of God has come to earth to be a little boy."

All: Rejoice and celebrate! Jesus, our Savior, has come!

Reader: It's Christmas Day! We celebrate the coming of a King. He came to set his children free, and that is why we sing.

All: Rejoice and celebrate! Jesus, our Savior, has come!

—Reader's words 1980, © 1987, Bert Witvoet. Calvinist Contact, 261 Martindale Road, Unit 4, St. Catharines, ON L2W 1A1, Canada; 416-682-8311. Used by permission.

Leader: Sing a new song to the LORD. He has done wonderful things.

Group: Sing to the Lord with joy!

Leader: [Sing) to the LORD with joy, everyone on earth. Burst into joyful songs and make music.

Group: Sing to the Lord with joy!

Leader: Make music to the LORD with the harp. Sing and make music with the harp.

Group: Sing to the Lord with joy!

Leader: Blow the trumpets. Give a blast on the ram's horn. [Sing) to the LORD with joy. He is the King.

Group: "Joy to the World"

—Based on Psalm 98:1, 4-6, New International Reader's Version (NIrV)

LEADER TIP

For a variation of this response, divide your group into two groups. Have Group A say the response as written; have Group B echo the response. If your group knows all four stanzas of "Joy to the World" (p. 110), sing one stanza following each group response. If you wish, add instruments group members have made. (We've included directions on p. 78 in the craft section for making shofars.) Or have your group present the psalm as a responsive reading for a worship service where instrumentalists play the harp, trumpet, and coronet.

One or more of these readings on pages 43-47 can be added to your praise and worship time during a regular Christmas session or they can be used as part of a Christmas program celebration. If some of your friends are good readers, be sure to involve them in this way.

LEADER TIP

A CHRISTMAS PRAYER

At Christmas, may our Savior
enfold you in his love.
and may he fill this season
with blessings from above.

Through all the days that
    follow,
may Christ be at your side—
an ever-present comfort,
a constant help and guide.

—Bernice E. Tilson, *Standard Christmas Program Book,* No. 36, page 17. © 1975, The Standard Publishing Co., Cincinnati, OH.

—Adapted from *Christmas Program Builder* No. 26, page 8, compiled by Grace Ramquist. © 1973, Lillenas Publishing Co., Kansas City, MO 64141.

GOD'S GIFT

At Christmastime the carols ring
so clearly through the frosty air.
God's people are rejoicing
and hearts are filled with prayer.

Christmas is a blessed day—
a day of gladness too,
for on that day God sent his
    Son—
his gift to me and you.

LEADER TIP

Make photocopies of one or both of these prayers to use as a greeting card to your friends or for them to give to others. Plan the layout so that you can get two cards from a sheet of red or green cardstock. Provide stickers, bits of old greeting cards, ribbon, and so on for your friends to decorate the outside of the cards. (See the craft activity section for other ideas.)

JESUS IS BORN!

Based on Luke 2:1-20

"We must go to Bethlehem,"
said Joseph to Mary one day.
So they packed their things and began to walk
to that city far away.
The trip was long—and Mary grew tired—
her baby was on its way.
But when they got to Bethlehem
they found no place to stay.

The innkeeper looked at Joseph
and slowly shook his head.
He stopped and looked outside—
then he pointed to a shed.
"There's a place that's warm and dry,
you could stay there instead."
So the tired pair settled there
and spread out some hay for a bed.

Mary's little one—God's own Son—
was born in the shed that night!
She wrapped her child in clean, warm cloth
and held him, oh, so tight,
while Joseph filled the manger bed
with hay so dry and light.
The thankful pair bowed their heads in prayer
to God for this special night.

And out in the fields near Bethlehem
bright angels came to earth
to sing to sleepy shepherds
the news of Jesus' birth.
The shepherds listened closely,
then quickly ran to see
the little one—God's own Son—
who was born for you and me!

—*I Learn About Jesus,* LiFE P&K/2, © 1994, 1998, CRC Publications

ONE STARRY NIGHT

Based on Matthew 2:1-12

Up in the sky one starry night,
a new star shone—especially bright!
The Magi knew God put it there
for them to follow if they cared.

"We care, we do!" the Magi said
to the star that twinkled overhead.
"For God has sent you to lead the way—
we'll bring fine gifts, we'll leave today!"

They followed the star a long, long way,
day and night, night and day—
until they reached Jerusalem,
where mean King Herod greeted them.

"You search for a king? How can it be?
I am the king—there's no one but me!"
Herod was angry, he wore a sad frown.
He wasn't about to give up his crown!

He sent his men to check in their books,
and off they hurried with worried looks.
Soon they were back to announce a strange thing—
it would happen in Bethlehem. Yes, a new king!

So the Magi set off on their journey again—
and the star brought them straight to Bethlehem.
Above Jesus' home it shone its light.
Their journey was over—O happy night!

They brought their gifts, they brought their love,
for they knew this King came from above.
The Magi's hearts were filled with joy
as they worshiped God's Son, the little boy.

—Abstracted from *Jesus' Miracles and Ministry,* LIFE 1&2/2, © 1994, 1998, CRC Publications

"THANK YOU, GOD"

"Thank you, God, for baby Jesus."
No bed to lay down his head—
Mary laid him in the manger
where the sheep and cattle fed.

"Thank you, God, for the angels."
They came down to earth
to tell the lowly shepherds
of the Christ child's birth.

"Thank you, God for the shepherds."
They came from the fields near Bethlehem
and found the baby in a manger
just as the angels told them.

"Thank you, God, for the wise men."
They followed the light of the star
to find God's promised king.
They brought gifts from the east so far.

"Thank you, God, for Jesus, our Savior."
Your love is for everyone—
that's the good news of Christmas.
Thank you, God, for giving us your Son.

LEADER TIP

If this poem is too difficult for most of your friends to read or recite, treat the first line as a response. Say the first line of each verse yourself, have the group echo the words; then read the rest of the verse.

Or provide simple costumes and props for volunteers to play the parts of Mary, the angels, shepherds, and wise men. Help them portray still-life scenes of the verses; focus a spotlight on each scene as you read the corresponding verse.

WISE MEN WORSHIP

Wise men came to Bethlehem
led by a brightly shining star.
Bringing gifts of gold, incense, and myrrh,
they traveled long and far.

They found Mary and the child—
Jesus, God's own Son.
They knelt and worshiped him,
Christ, the promised one.

We too should worship him,
for Christ is still the King.
Let's sing and praise his name,
with joy our voices ring.

LEADER TIP

Ahead of time, copy the heart, bell, angel, star, and Christmas ball patterns (pp. 137-140) on various colors of cardstock. (You'll want one ornament for each person in your group.) If you wish, have friends and mentors decorate the ornaments (see welcome activity on p. 34). Or simply punch a hole in the top of each ornament and make a loop hanger of narrow red and green ribbon; distribute randomly to group members.

Set up an undecorated Christmas tree in the center of your praise and worship area. Invite friends and mentors to come forward to hang their ornaments as you lead the worship time. Sing the suggested songs (see songs section, pp. 99-121), or choose other carols that are familiar to your group.

Leader: Come one, come all to the Christmas tree. So tall, it points our hearts to God above. Come one, come all to hear and see the story it tells of Jesus and his love. **(Invite group to hang hearts on tree.)**

Song: "He Came Down"

Leader: The bells ring out the story of a manger filled with hay—where Jesus, God's Son, our Savior was laid on Christmas Day. **(Invite group to hang bells on tree.)**

Song: "Ring the Bells"

Leader: The angels' happy voices said, "Peace to God's people on earth." To the shepherds in the fields, they told of our dear Savior's birth. **(Invite group to hang angels on tree.)**

Song: "Angels We Have Heard on High" (stanza 1) or "Gloria/Glory"

Leader: God placed a bright and shining star to guide the wise men on their way. Across the desert and the hills afar, they found the place where Jesus lay. **(Invite group to hang stars on tree.)**

Song: "We Three Kings" (chorus)

Leader: All around the world this day, we celebrate the birthday of a baby boy—Jesus came to take our sins away and fills our hearts with hope and love and joy. **(Invite group to hang Christmas balls on tree.)**

Song: "Joy to the World"

Leader: On the hills of Bethlehem shepherds watched their flocks by night. The sky was clear, the sheep so still when suddenly appeared a glorious light.

Song: "While Shepherds Watched" (stanza 1)

Leader: An angel came to comfort them, proclaimed the birth of Christ the King. "Fear not," the heavenly angel said, "for tidings of great joy I bring."

Song: "While Shepherds Watched" (stanza 2)

Leader: "For unto you has come a Savior, born in Bethlehem's stable stall. There you will find the baby sleeping—in a manger bed, a baby small."

Song: "Away in a Manger" (stanza 1)

Leader: The shepherds went and found the baby just as the angels had foretold. They worshiped him with joy and gladness; their hearts were filled with joy untold.

Song: "Joy to the World" (stanza 1)

Leader: The shepherds told everyone the story of the precious Christ child's birth. We too must tell the story of salvation—proclaim God's love to all the earth.

Song: "Go Tell It on the Mountain" (chorus)

—Adapted from Marilyn A. Smith, *Christmas Programs for Church Groups.* © 1968, Baker Book House, Grand Rapids, Mich. Used by permission.

For permission to photocopy for local Friendship program use contact Baker Book House Company, P.O. Box 6287, Grand Rapids, MI 49516-6287; 616-676-9185; 616-676-9573 (fax).

LEADER TIP

Purchase or borrow a nativity set with fairly large movable figures. Involve friends and mentors in placing the figures in the nativity scene as you read the narration and Scripture. (Or, if you prefer, have friends and mentors dressed in simple costumes portray the scene.) Invite the group to sing the suggested songs (see songs section, pp. 99-121). Note that the songs are familiar carols your group probably already knows, or else they have repetitive phrases that are easy to learn.

Leader: This is the story of Christmas **(place stable in the center of your worship area where everyone can see it; open your Bible to read):**

"Today in the town of David a Savior has been born to you. He is Christ the Lord" (Luke 2:11).

Song: O Little Town of Bethlehem" (stanza 1)

Leader Joseph and Mary **(add figures)** had gone to Bethlehem to be counted.

While Joseph and Mary were there, the time came for the child to be born. She gave birth to her first baby. It was a boy (v. 6).

Song: "Mary Had a Baby" (stanza 1)

Leader: A baby boy!

[Mary) wrapped him in large strips of cloth. Then she placed him in a manger. **(Add baby Jesus in manger.)** *There was no room for them in the inn* (v. 7).

Song: "Mary Had a Baby" (stanzas 4, 5, 2, 3)

Leader: Jesus, God's Son, our Savior, had come. Who would hear the good news first? **(Place shepherds and sheep outside the stable.)**

There were shepherds living out in the fields nearby. It was night, and they were looking after their sheep. An angel of the Lord appeared to them. **(Place angel near shepherds.)** *And the glory of the Lord shone around them* (vv. 8-9).

Song: "While Shepherds Watched" (stanza 1)

Leader: The shepherds were afraid.

But the angel said to them, "Do not be afraid. I bring you good news of great joy. It is for all the people. Today in the town of David a Savior has been born to you. He is Christ the Lord. Here is how you will know I am telling you the truth. You will find a baby wrapped in strips of cloth and lying in a manger" (vv. 10-12).

Song: "Good News"

Leader: Suddenly the shepherds saw the sky fill with angels. **(Add additional angels if they're part of the nativity set.)** They were praising God and saying:

"May glory be given to God in the highest heaven! And may peace be given to those he is pleased with on earth!" (v. 14).

Song: "Angels We Have Heard on High" (chorus) or "Gloria"

Leader: When the angels went back to heaven, the shepherds said to one another,

"Let's go to Bethlehem. Let's see this thing that has happened, which the Lord has told us about" (v. 15).

Song: "Angels We Have Heard on High" (stanzas 1 and 3)

Leader: The shepherds hurried to Bethlehem and found Mary and Joseph and the baby. After they saw Jesus, they told everyone about the Savior.

They gave glory and praise to God. Everything they had seen and heard was just as they had been told (v. 20).

Song: "Go Tell It on the Mountain" (chorus)

Leader: This is the story of Christmas **(join hands around the nativity scene):**

"Today in the town of David a Savior has been born to you. He is Christ the Lord" (v. 11).

—Scripture from Luke 2:1-20, New International Reader's Version (NIrV)

—Adapted from drama developed by Bette Bosma for her Friendship Club, Second Christian Reformed Church, Grand Haven, MI. Used by permission.

Friends will benefit from visiting a live nativity presentation. (Check your local newspapers or with Christian radio stations.) You'll want to make sure that the entire journey is accessible to those with limited mobility or in wheelchairs. It might be best to take small groups at different times rather than your entire group at once. Depending on the amount of dialogue and acting presented, be prepared to tell the story so that your friends will understand.

LEADER TIP

Leader: The angels filled the sky with light; the shepherds saw it all around them. They heard good news that quiet night: "For to you a Savior is born in Bethlehem."

Group: Praise God, Jesus is born! **(Lift hands in praise, sign "Jesus.")**

Leader: The shepherds hurried straightaway to see that which the angels had told them. They found the babe who in a manger lay—they knew Jesus their Savior had come!

Group: Praise God, Jesus is born! **(Lift hands in praise, sign "Jesus.")**

Leader: Jesus came that day for everyone. God kept this promise true: Jesus, the Savior of the world, God's Son is God's gift to me and you!

Group: Praise God, Jesus is born! **(Lift hands in praise, sign "Jesus.")**

All: Thank you, God, for Jesus! **(Fold hands, bow heads.)**

LEADER TIP   You'll find directions for signing "Jesus" on page 111.

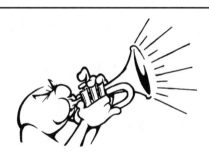

Dramas

- Come to Bethlehem
- The Little Shepherd Boy
- Shepherd's Story Puzzle
- "Today, a Savior Is Born!"

LEADER TIP

In this section, we've included dramas that range in difficulty from easy to more complex. You may wish to use these for performance or simply as a night to act out and enjoy the Christmas story. Consider using one or more of these dramas for the Sunday school program, involving your Friendship group with children and youth from the congregation.

In many cases, the cast of characters can be decreased or enlarged to meet the needs of your group. When assigning roles, keep in mind your friends' abilities. Some friends may have speaking parts; others may have walk-on parts or play parts of the scenery, such as stars. Make sure your friends are comfortable in their roles.

Keep costumes simple. Large bath towels or pieces of colorful fabric clipped at the neck with clothespins make tunics for shepherds and other male characters. Large T-shirts work as tunics and robes for youth.

White sheets can be draped to make angel robes. (Or use choir robes or bathrobes for all costumes, adding colorful cord for belts.) Squares of white or colorful fabric folded to make a triangle can be wrapped around the head and tied in back. (Solicit old sheets and unused fabric from members of your church family.)

Unless otherwise indicated, permission to photocopy materials in this section for local Friendship program use is granted by CRC Publications.

Cast

- Joseph
- Mary
- Angel(s)
- Shepherds
- Wise Men

Costumes

- Long tunics and head wraps for Joseph and the shepherds
- Long dress for Mary
- White robes for angel(s)
- Robes and crowns for wise men (crown pattern on p. 141)

Props

- Large cardboard or wood frames (3)
- Large star with lights
- Heavy wire (optional)
- Bales of hay
- Manger box
- Baby doll
- Chair
- Bible (NIrV)
- Shepherds' staffs
- Gift boxes, bottles
- Spotlight

LEADER TIP

This drama centers around six scenes portrayed as still-life pictures behind three large frames. Construct the frames of cardboard or wood, approximately 6' (2 m) square. (Make the frames longer if your cast is large.) Add braces to the frames so that they will stand straight up and sturdy.

Place the three frames in your stage area, allowing some distance between them. (You may also need to secure the top of the frame to the ceiling with heavy wire.) Add bales of hay to the center frame to steady it and create the manger scene. Hang a large star above the center frame. (Use a star already decorated with lights, or construct the star of heavy cardboard, and carefully tape or staple a string of white lights to the star.) Place a manger box with baby doll in the center frame and a chair in the frame to the right of the center frame.

The cast can be kept quite small or expanded with a host of angels and several shepherds. You'll want the costumes for the wise men to look more elegant than those of the shepherds; provide crowns for their heads. (See tips on p. 53 for simple costumes and crown pattern on p. 141.)

Narration and singing accompany the scenes and offer a good way to involve group members who are not part of the cast. Or you may wish to have the audience sing along. We suggest that you invite a soloist to sing all three stanzas of "Angels We Have Heard on High." (See songs section, pp. 99-121)

Before the drama begins, actors take their places and stand motionless—shepherds and one or more angels in the frame to the left of center, Mary and Joseph in center frame, and wise men in frame to the right of center. (Shepherds will move to the center frame for scene 4, and Mary will move to the frame with the wise men for scene 5. All others will remain in place.) As the drama begins, a spotlight focuses on the star above the center frame.

The script follows:

Scene 1

[Spotlight focuses on star above center frame.]

Narrator: Long ago the prophet Micah said **(read from Bible):**

> *"Bethlehem, you might not be an important town in the nation of Judah. But out of you will come a ruler over Israel for me."* (Micah 5:2)

God promised that Jesus, the Savior, would come to Bethlehem.

Song: "O Little Town of Bethlehem" (stanza 1)

Scene 2

[Spotlight focuses on Mary and Joseph standing by the manger. Baby doll is lying in the manger.]

Narrator: One day, the governor made a law that all the people in the land should be counted. Joseph said, "Come, Mary, we must go to Bethlehem." Mary was expecting a baby.

When Mary and Joseph came to Bethlehem, there was no room for them in the inn. Joseph begged the innkeeper for a place for Mary to rest. Finally, the innkeeper showed them the stable where the cattle were feeding. That night, baby Jesus was born in Bethlehem. Mary wrapped him in strips of cloth and laid him in the manger. The Savior had come to Bethlehem!

Song: "Away in a Manger" (stanza 1)

Scene 3

[Spotlight focuses on one or more angels talking to several shepherds in the frame to the left of center.]

Narrator: The shepherds in the fields near Bethlehem were the first to know about Jesus' birth. They were watching their sleepy sheep when suddenly they were surrounded with a bright light! An angel appeared! The shepherds were shaking with fear, but the angel said **(read from Bible):**

> *"Do not be afraid. I bring you good news of great joy. it is for all the people. Today in the town of David a Savior has been born to you. He is Christ the Lord."* (Luke 2:10-11)

And then the sky filled with angels, singing "Glory to God in the highest. And peace to men on earth."

Solo: "Angels We Have Heard on High" (stanzas 1-2) *or* "Hark! the Herald Angels Sing" (stanza 1) *or* "Gloria"

Scene 4

[Shepherds move to manger frame. Spotlight focuses on the shepherds kneeling before the baby in the manger as Mary and Joseph look on.]

Narrator: "Come, let's go to Bethlehem," the shepherds said to each other. There they found the baby lying in a manger, wrapped in cloths—just as the angel said.

Solo: "Angels We Have Heard on High" (stanza 3)

Narrator: The shepherds went home and told everyone what they had seen and heard.

Scene 5

[Mary moves to frame with wise men. Spotlight focuses on star, then on Mary, seated on a chair, holding the baby doll. Wise men are kneeling, offering gifts and worshiping.]

Narrator: After Jesus was born, wise men came from the East looking for the newborn King. They had seen his star and wanted to worship this king. They followed the star until it came to Bethlehem to the place where Jesus was.

When they saw Jesus, they bowed down and worshiped him. They gave him gifts—gold, incense, and myrrh.

Song: "We Three Kings" (stanza 1)

Scene 6

[Mary moves back to manger frame. Spotlight focuses on Mary and Joseph standing in front of the manger. Mary is holding the baby.]

Narrator: Mary and Joseph came to Bethlehem to be counted. Jesus came to Bethlehem to be the Savior of the world. Shepherds came to see the baby in the manger. Wise men came to worship the King. Let us come to Bethlehem too—let us worship Christ the Lord!

[As the narrator invites everyone to come to Bethlehem, the group comes forward and joins hands in a semicircle in front of the manger scene.]

Song: "O Come, All Ye Faithful" (stanza 1)

Narrator: Go now, like the shepherds, to tell the good news that Jesus is born.

[Group returns to seats as they sing.]

Song: "Go, Tell It on the Mountain" (chorus)

—Adapted from drama written by Friendship leaders, First Christian Reformed Church, Sheboygan, Wisconsin. Scripture passages from New International Reader's Version (NIrV).

LEADER TIP

If building the three frames and setting them up presents a bigger challenge than you're ready for, simply designate three distinct areas for characters to portray the scenes. The spotlight will provide a framing effect. No spotlight? You can use a filmstrip projector or a slide projector as your spotlight.

Cast
- Joseph
- Mary
- Angels
- Shepherds
- Little Shepherd Boy

Costumes
- Long tunics and head wraps for Joseph and the shepherds
- Long dress for Mary
- White robes for angels
- Small tunic for little shepherd boy

Props
- Manger
- Baby doll
- Shepherd staffs
- Spotlight
- White sheets (optional)

LEADER TIP

This is a simple drama presented as still-life scenes with some limited movement. Cast members and props will be in place for the first two scenes as the drama begins. The spotlight will focus on each scene individually as the reader describes the story the two scenes portray; then the spotlight follows the little shepherd boy from scene 2 to scene 1. Involve as many in your group as you wish, increasing the number of angels and shepherds to fit your group and available space. (See tip on p. 53 for simple costumes.)

If you wish to show the scenes as silhouettes rather than in color, hang white sheets across the back of your stage area. Have the characters stand in front of the sheets to portray each scene; shine the spotlight from behind each scene.

The script follows:

Scene 1
[Mary and Joseph stand close to the manger in which the baby doll is placed. Mary lifts the baby from the manger and cradles it in her arms as the spotlight shines on the scene.]

Narrator: Born this night was Mary's baby boy. Our Savior, Jesus, he was named. He brought peace, goodwill, and joy—God's love to all the world proclaimed.

Scene 2
[Angels with arms lifted in praise surround the kneeling shepherds, who are afraid. The little shepherd boy rises to his feet as the spotlight shines on the scene.]

Narrator: "Fear not," the host of angels said. The shepherds heard their message ring: "In Bethelehem, you'll find a baby in a manger bed." They went to worship him, the newborn king.

From Scene 2 to Scene 1

[Mary has placed the doll back in the manager. The little shepherd boy moves from scene 2 to scene 1 as the spotlight follows him. He kneels by the manager.]

Narrator: "Look," said the little shepherd boy as he knelt by the manger filled with hay. "This babe in cloths will bring us joy. I'll tell the good news this very day!"

LEADER TIP	If you wish, sing one stanza from selected Christmas carols as the spotlight continues to focus on each scene:

- *Scene 1:* "Mary Had a Baby" (p. 111), "Away in a Manger" (p. 102), "O Little Town of Bethlehem" (p. 113)

- *Scene 2:* "Hark the Herald Angels Sing" (p. 108), "Angels We Have Heard on High" (p. 101), "Gloria/Glory" (p. 104), "While Shepherds Watched" (p. 121)

- *From Scene 2 to Scene 1:* "Joy to the World" (p. 110), "Good News" (p. 105), "Go, Tell It on the Mountain" (p. 107)

Cast

- Old shepherd (narrator)
- Angels
- Joseph
- Shepherds
- Mary
- Sheep
- Baby
- Star
- Manger
- Wise Men
- Animals
- Gifts

Costumes

- Long tunic and head wrap for old shepherd (narrator)
- Head wraps for the shepherds and Joseph
- Shawl for Mary
- Bunting for baby
- Cardboard box for manger costume
- Animal masks or signs (photocopied from patterns on pp. 131-134)
- Star headband or sign for the star (photocopied from pattern on p. 148)
- Crown headbands for wise men (photocopied from pattern on p. 141)
- Bow headbands or signs for the gifts (photocopied from pattern on p. 135)
- Garland halos for angels

Props

- Baby doll
- Masking tape outline of Bethlehem
- Folding chairs as needed
- Shepherd's staff

LEADER TIP

Using this drama as an impromptu way to tell the story is a great way to involve your entire group and to include family members and others who come to celebrate with you. Each person will be a character, animal, or object that fits into the shepherd's Christmas story puzzle.

Provide a long tunic, head wrap, and a staff for the old shepherd who will narrate the story. Use squares of white or colored fabric folded in triangles and tied in the back as head wraps for the shepherds and Joseph. Provide a soft shawl for Mary to wrap around her head and a blanket for the baby doll she carries. For the manger, cut part of the top from a cardboard box, leaving enough of the box to hang on the shoulders of the person playing the manger. For the angels' halos, tape or staple lengths of gold or silver Christmas garland to form a circle around their heads.

Costumes for all the others will be various types of headbands or masks. (If you think your group will be uncomfortable wearing headbands and masks, you can make signs from the same patterns to be worn around the neck or carried.)

Consider involving teens or senior members of your church family in making the star, crowns, bows, and masks. (You'll need one star, three crowns, three bows, and as many masks as you assign people to play the parts of the sheep and animals.)

Photocopy the star pattern and extension on page 148 on yellow cardstock. Outline the star with glitter or gold Christmas rope. Tape or staple the extension to the star headband, fitting it to the wearer.

Make three photocopies of the crown pattern and the extension on page 141. (Copy on yellow cardstock.) If you wish, add stickers, beads, or buttons to decorate the crown. Tape or staple the extension to the crown, fitting it to the wearer.

Make three photocopies of the bow pattern and extension on page 135. (Copy on three different bright colors of cardstock.) Tape or staple the extension to the bow, fitting the headband to the wearer.

Make masks for the sheep and animals (donkey, cow, mouse) by photocopying the patterns on pages 131-134 on white and tan cardstock. Cut out the eyes, nose, and mouth. Tape or staple a band of narrow elastic to each side of the mask. If you wish, add cotton balls to the sheep and strings of black or brown yarn to the donkey and cow faces.

With masking tape, make an outline of the city of Bethlehem on the floor in your meeting area. You'll need a space large enough to for every person to fit into the puzzle. Be sure to allow room for walkers, crutches, and wheelchairs, and provide folding chairs for those who cannot stand for very long. Your outline (puzzle frame) might look something like the illustration on page 61 (group members will fill in the puzzle on cue from the old shepherd).

You'll find the music for the songs on pages 99-121 in the back of this book. Have the old shepherd lead the singing or let an accompanist give the cue.

The script follows:

Song: "O Come, All Ye Faithful"

[Cast enters in the order listed on p. 59. They stand off to the side waiting for their turn to fill in the puzzle.]

Old shepherd: It's been a long, long time since that first Christmas night. I'm an old shepherd now, but I remember so well what the angels said the night our Savior was born in Bethlehem. **(Shepherd sings a few lines of "Gloria/Glory.")**

I can see the little town of Bethlehem in my mind. It's like a giant jigsaw puzzle where all the pieces fit together to make a beautiful picture of Christmas. **(Old shepherd walks around the outline of Bethlehem, hums part of "O Little Town of Bethlehem." He steps inside and remains inside the puzzle outline, directing the cast where to position themselves.)**

The stable stood right here. Because there was no room in the inn, Joseph and Mary spent the night in the stable. Jesus, our Savior, was born here in Bethlehem—in a stable. **(Joseph and Mary, carrying baby doll, take their place in the center of the puzzle.)** Mary laid her baby boy in a manger—just a wooden box filled with hay. **(Manger enters, sits cross-legged in front of Joseph and Mary.)**

Songs: "Away in a Manger" (stanza 1)
"Silent Night" (stanza 1)

Old shepherd: "The cattle were lowing" . . . **(shepherd sings first line of second stanza of "Away in a Manger").** That's right—the animals in the stable welcomed the baby named Jesus. **(Animals enter, stand behind and off to the side of Joseph and Mary and the manger.)**

Oh, I remember the night. It was so cold and quiet on the hills near Bethlehem. I was a young shepherd boy, helping my older sister watch our father's sheep. There were other shepherds and sheep all around us. **(Shepherds and sheep enter and take their place off to one corner of the puzzle outline. Sheep sit with heads lowered. Shepherds and old shepherd sit down among the sheep.)**

I was almost asleep, when suddenly a bright light shone all around us. I jumped to my feet. **(Shepherds jump up, sheep lift heads.)** I couldn't believe my eyes. An angel **(one angel enters and stands near old shepherd)** said, "Don't be afraid. I bring you good news. Today a Savior is born Bethlehem. He is Christ the Lord."

And then suddenly a large group of angels **(other angels surround the shepherds and sheep)** were all around us. What a beautiful sight! What a beautiful praise they brought! Listen—I can hear it still!

Song: "Gloria/Glory"

Old shepherd: When the angels left, the shepherds said, "We must go to Bethlehem!" So we hurried to Bethlehem **(old shepherd rushes toward the manger)** and found the newborn baby wrapped in cloths, lying in a manger—just as the angel said. God had kept the promise—God had sent a Savior, born in Bethlehem.

That was good news—too good to keep to ourselves. After we had seen the baby Jesus, we told everyone what we had seen and heard.

Song: "Joy to the World" (stanza 1)

Old shepherd: Later, wise men in the East saw a bright star in the sky and came to find the child who was born to be the king of God's people. **(Star takes position in right corner of puzzle. Wise men follow in single file behind the star.)** The star led the wise men to the house where Jesus was. When they saw Jesus with his mother, Mary, they bowed down **(wise men kneel)** and worshiped him. They brought gifts **(gifts enter, sit down in front of wise men)** of gold, incense, and myrrh.

Song: "We Three Kings" (stanza 1)

Old shepherd: (walks around outside of puzzle) I'm an old man now, but I'll never forget this picture of Christmas. The story of Christmas lives in my heart: Jesus, the baby born in Bethlehem, came to be my Savior and King. Jesus came to give us life. We must let the whole world know the Christmas story!

Song: "Ring the Bells"

"Today, a Savior Is Born!"

Cast
- Caesar Augustus
- Shepherds
- Joseph
- Angels
- Mary

Costumes
- Toga for Caesar Augustus
- Long tunics and head wraps for Joseph and shepherds
- Long tunic for Mary
- White robes and halos for angels

Props
- Microphone
- Scroll
- Spotlights (optional)
- Manger
- Strips of cloth
- Recorded music, CD player (optional)
- Doll
- Drum or trumpet (optional)
- Staffs for shepherds

LEADER TIP

This drama is intended to be performed for an audience, probably your friends' family members and caregivers. Friends will represent the characters (Mary and Joseph, the shepherds and the angels) and pantomime their parts. Everyone—including those with physical limitations and those who are nonverbal—should have a part. (Someone in a wheelchair would be thrilled to play the part of Mary!) If you need additional characters, involve mentors and adults and children from the audience. If your group is large, present the drama twice, each time with a different cast.

The script is read by a narrator, who will stand at a microphone placed off to the side of the "stage" area. If you have time to practice, and if your friends are able, have the angels and the shepherds speak their lines.

Costumes should be simple. Lengths of fabric wrapped around the body to form tunics work well, even for those in wheelchairs. Use a sheet for the emperor's toga and tie it in place with a bright-colored rope.

Instrumental music (piano, guitar, and so on) between scenes is suggested in order to give adequate time for people to enter and exit the stage. (You could also use recorded music.) For the opening scene, use a real drum and trumpet or simply do a drum beat with rhythm instruments.

A raised stage area and two different entrance/exits will facilitate movement. The manger is placed center stage; doll and strips of cloth are hidden inside. While two spotlights (one on each side of the auditorium) are ideal, at minimum, house lights should be turned on and off. (Involve those in your church who usually take care of lighting for worship.) The shepherds should be in place in a darkened part of the stage as the drama begins.

The drama ends with the entire cast singing "Go, Tell It on the Mountain." You may wish to conclude the performance with the cast and audience singing one stanza of the carols used as background music (see songs section, pp. 99-121).

The script follows:

Narrator: A long time ago—over 2000 years, in fact—Caesar Augustus was the ruler of a faraway land.

[Drum roll or trumpet fanfare plays as friend dressed in a Roman toga enters the scene carrying a scroll. Spotlights focus on friend as he unrolls the scroll.]

Narrator: Caesar Augustus made a law. It said that a list had to be made of everyone in the whole Roman world. All the people in the land had to go to their own towns to be listed.

[Caesar Augustus exits as spotlights go off.]

Narrator: So Joseph went too. He went to Bethlehem with Mary to be listed. Mary was engaged to him. She was expecting a baby.

[Joseph and Mary enter on opposite side from Caesar Augustus. Spotlights focus on them.]

Narrator: It was a long way from their home in Nazareth to Bethlehem. They went there because Joseph belonged to the family of King David.

["O Little Town of Bethlehem" is played as Joseph and Mary walk slowly to center stage to the manger. Spotlights follow them. Joseph stands in front of the manger; Mary kneels down in front of it.]

Narrator: While Joseph and Mary were there, the time came for the child to be born. She gave birth to her first baby. It was a boy. She wrapped him in large strips of cloth. Then she placed him in a manger. There was no room for them in the inn.

[Mary unobtrusively picks up the doll and wraps it in cloths. She holds the wrapped baby in her arm as "Away in a Manger" is played. Lights fade out as the music ends. Mary and Joseph remain in place; Mary places baby in manger.]

Narrator: There were shepherds living out in the fields nearby. It was night, and they were looking after their sheep.

[Very dim lights shine on the stage area where the shepherds are in place as "While Shepherds Watched" is played. Shepherds move around a bit as though tending sheep.]

Narrator: An angel of the Lord appeared to them. And the glory of the Lord shone around them.

[Bright lights shine as one angel enters and approaches shepherds. Shepherds are startled and fall on their knees and faces.]

Narrator: The shepherds were afraid! But the angel said to them,

Angel or Narrator: Do not be afraid. I bring you good news of great joy. It is for all people. Today in the town of David a Savior has been born to you. He is Christ the Lord. Here is how you will know. . . . You will find a baby wrapped in strips of cloth and lying in a manger.

Narrator: Suddenly a large group of angels also appeared.

[Group of angels enter and join the one angel as "Hark! the Herald Angels Sing" is played. Bright lights focus on the group.]

Narrator: The angels were praising God. They said,

Angels or Narrator: Glory to God in heaven! Peace to people on earth.

[Angels leave through the same door they entered as "Gloria/Glory" is played. Spotlight follows, gradually dimming. Light refocuses on shepherds.]

Narrator: After the angels left, the shepherds said to one another,

Sheperds or Narrator: Let's go to Bethlehem. Let's see this thing that has happened, which the Lord has told us about.

[Spotlight follows shepherds to the manger as "O Come, All Ye Faithful" is played.]

Narrator: So they hurried off and found Mary and Joseph and the baby. The baby was lying in a manger.

[Mary picks up baby and shepherds kneel in front of the manger as "Mary Had a Baby" is played.]

Narrator: After the shepherds saw the baby, they told everyone about the baby. They reported what the angel had said about this child. All who heard it were amazed at what the shepherds said to them.

[Slowly shepherds leave the manger and return to their "fields." They're talking excitedly to each other. Spotlight follows, then fades away as "Go, Tell It on the Mountain" is played.]

Narrator: The shepherds went back to their sheep. They gave glory and praise to God. Everything they had seen and heard was just as the angels had told them.

[House lights come on as Caesar Augustus and angels reenter. Entire cast gathers around the manger and sings "Go, Tell It on the Mountain." Invite the audience to join them for the chorus and one or more stanzas.]

—Based on Luke 2:1-20, New International Reader's Version (NIrV).

Craft Activities

- Advent Calendar
- Advent Chain
- Advent Wreath
- Angels
- Candleholders
- Christmas Bells
- Christmas Stars

- Foil Star Ornaments
- Gift Wrap String Painting
- Glittery Tree Ornament
- Modeling Clay Créche
- Shofar (Horn)
- "Stained Glass" Nativity Scene
- Stamp Art Placemats

LEADER TIP

You can use these craft activities in a variety of ways during a regular session or for special gatherings with family and friends. Making the Advent wreath can be part of a praise and worship activity (see "Advent Worship Plans: Good News" (pp. 37-39) and "Advent Wreath: What Is Christmas?" p. 40). Your group might make bells and star ornaments to decorate your tree (see also Welcome Activities, pp. 30-35 and "The Christmas Tree's Story," p. 48).

Shofars and other homemade instruments can be used to accompany carol singing (see also "A Christmas Psalm," p. 42). You may also wish to make some of the crafts as gifts for family and friends.

Consider the interests and abilities of your friends when choosing craft activities. If necessary, do much of the tracing, cutting, and so on ahead of time, allowing your friends to complete the project and take pride in their own work.

Unless otherwise indicated, permission to photocopy materials in this section for local Friendship program use is granted by CRC Publications.

Materials

- Calendar (photocopied from pattern on p. 128)
- Calendar messages (photocopied from pattern on p. 129)
- White cardstock for calendar and calendar messages
- Embroidery scissors
- Markers, sidewalk chalk, or crayons
- Hair spray (optional)
- Small Christmas stickers or stars
- Ornaments, trim, and so on cut from old Christmas cards (optional)
- Glue

Directions

Ahead of time, photocopy the calendar and calendar messages on cardstock. (White will be the easiest to color and read.) Use a small embroidery scissors to cut the 24 doors open.

Provide markers, sidewalk chalk, or crayons for your friends to color the nativity scene. (If you use chalk, spray the finished picture with hair spray to keep the chalk from rubbing off.) Help them place a Christmas sticker or star on each of the doors, forming a decorative border at the top and bottom of the calendar. (If you prefer, provide a collection of small bows, bells, ornaments, stars, and so on cut from old Christmas cards. Glue one piece on each door.) Finished calendars will look something like this:

Run a border of glue around the Christmas message page and carefully place the calendar page over the top. Show your friends how to open one door each day and do the activity described.

LEADER TIP

If your friends are nonreaders, you might want to omit the calendar message page. Simply send the stickers home with them and encourage them to put one sticker on one door every day before Christmas. When they finish, they'll have a cheerful Christmas calendar—and it will be Christmas Day!

Materials

- 1" (2.5 cm) strips of red and green cardstock or construction paper
- Christmas stickers and stars
- Ziplock bags
- Marker
- Clear tape or stapler

Directions

This is a good activity for the week after Thanksgiving. Ahead of time, cut strips of red and green cardstock or construction paper so that you have enough for each person. (Each person will need one strip and Christmas sticker or star for each day until Christmas.) If possible, try to find some stickers of the nativity figures. Assemble each person's supplies in a Ziplock bag.

Explain that the fourth Sunday before Christmas marks the beginning of *Advent,* the time of waiting for Jesus' birthday. Invite your friends to make a chain to help them count off the days before Christmas. Show them how to stick a Christmas sticker or star to the middle of each strip of paper. Number the strips with a marker. Assemble the chain, stickers to the outside as you tape or staple the loops together. Encourage your friends to hang their chains (with day one at the bottom) somewhere where they will remember to remove one link each day before Christmas.

Optional Activity

The Advent chain can become a prayer chain. Complete the strips as described above. On the back of each strip, write a name or short prayer request (or draw a simple picture) to remind your friends to pray for specific people and needs each day of the Advent season. (If praying for others is part of your meeting together, you'll probably have quite a list. Give your friend an opportunity to name or describe other specific needs as well.)

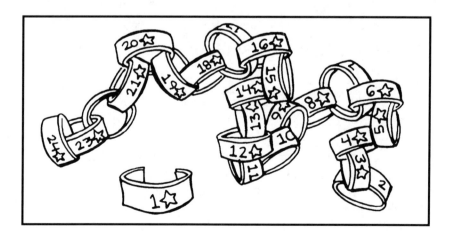

Materials

- Purple taper candles (3)
- Pink taper candle
- White taper candle
- 12" (30 cm) Styrofoam wreath
- Table knife or dowel
- Glue (optional)
- Plastic or live greens or garland
- Florist pins or hairpins
- Purple ribbon

Directions

Use a table knife or a dowel slightly smaller in diameter than the candles to make five holes evenly spaced around the circle. (Remember to make the holes slightly smaller than the base of the candles so that the candle will fit snugly. For added safety, run a bead of glue around the base of the candle before inserting the candles in the holes.)

Cut greens into small lengths and secure to the base with florist pins or hairpins. Attach a large purple bow as shown.

We've used the Advent wreath as the focal point for the Advent worship plans on pages 37-39 and for the Advent wreath activity on page 40. At some point—perhaps as you make the wreath—you will want to explain the meaning of the wreath. Here's a simple explanation: **LEADER TIP**

- The evergreens remind us that God never changes and that Jesus gives us new life.
- The candles remind us that Jesus is the Light of the world.
- The circle-shaped wreath tells us that God is eternal; God has no beginning or end.
- The purple candles remind us to prepare for Jesus' birthday.
- The pink candle tells us that the joy of Christmas is near.
- The white candle is the Christ candle to remind us that Jesus, the perfect Son of God, is the reason for Christmas.

Materials

- Angel pattern pieces (photocopied from pattern on p. 130)
- White cardstock for angels
- Clear tape
- Glue or double-faced tape
- Glitter or glitter glue (optional)
- Fine-tipped black markers
- Narrow white ribbon (optional)

Directions

Photocopy and cut out the three angel pattern pieces. Wrap the body piece (the semi-circle) around to form a cone; tape in place. If you wish,

rub with glitter glue or add glitter to the angel's halo. Glue the wing/halo piece behind the cone as shown (or use a strip of double-faced tape). Invite your friend to draw facial features in the circle of the remaining angel pattern piece. (The expressions will delight everyone!) Glue or tape the face piece to the cone to complete the angel. If you want to use the angels as tree ornaments, glue a loop of white ribbon to the back of the wings.

Materials

- Scraps of 2 x 4 and 2 x 6 lumber (blocks or odd shapes)
- Electric drill with 3/4" bit
- Newspapers
- Plastic gloves
- Paint shirts
- Sandpaper
- Stain
- Rags
- Small brushes
- Old Christmas cards
- Glue
- Clear sealer
- Red and green taper candles
- Bows and greens (optional)
- Florist wire (optional)

Directions

Ahead of time, drill one hole a bit smaller than the base of candles in the center of each scrap of wood. (If some of your friends enjoy working with wood, invite them to help with this step, or ask a boys' club or senior members of your congregation to help.)

Cover your work area with newspapers and provide plastic gloves and paint shirts. Offer your friends sandpaper to smooth the edges of the

blocks. Show them how to brush stain over the block and quickly rub it off with rags. Let the stain dry.

At a later time, provide a selection of old Christmas cards (or pieces of cards you've cut out ahead of time). Show your friends how to glue card pieces to the sides of the wood blocks. Brush or spray clear sealer over the entire block. Allow to dry.

Insert the candle. If you wish, use florist wire to attach a bow and artificial greens around the base of the candle.

LEADER TIP

If you choose to make these candleholders, carefully think through the steps. Do as much ahead of time as necessary, but allow your friends to do as much of the finishing as possible. Be sure to allow drying time between the staining and sealing steps. (If you find the staining too messy, simply spray with clear sealer.)

Use the candleholders to decorate the table for a Christmas party or for gifts. (For gift bags, decorate brown lunch bags with bits of Christmas cards or with stamp art—see directions on p. 81.)

Materials

- Plastic communion cups
- Drill or wood-burning tool
- Fishing line
- Large and small colored beads
- Glue
- Glitter
- Plastic punch cups
- Jingle bells
- Ribbon
- Fresh or artificial evergreens

Directions

Ahead of time, drill holes in the ends of plastic communion cups. (Or use a wood-burning tool to make a hole.) Use the hand-over-hand technique to help your friend thread fishing line through a large colored bead. Then

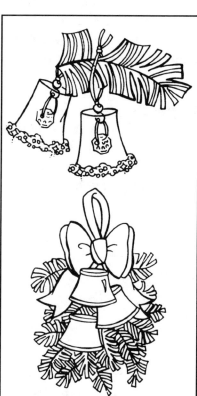

slip both ends of the thread through a smaller bead and knot. Run line up through hole in cup, place another small bead on top of the cup and knot again. To form a hanger, make another knot about 2" (5 cm) above the bead; clip evenly. Dip edges of cup into glue and then into glitter. Let dry.

To make larger bells, use plastic punch cups instead of the communion cups. Use a jingle bell instead of the large colored bead; complete the bells as described above. Arrange these larger bells with greens and ribbon to hang on a door.

—Adapted from Verna Harris, "An Evening of Christmas Crafts," *Creative Ideas for Advent,* Vol. 3, page 47, edited by Linda Davidson. Educational Ministries, Inc., Prescott, Arizona.

LEADER TIP
Check the welcome activities section (pp. 34-35) for other ideas for making Christmas ornaments.

Materials

- Craft (popsicle) sticks
- Glue
- Glue gun (optional)
- Markers, highlighters, star stickers, glitter
- Permanent black marker (optional)
- Narrow red or green ribbon

Directions

Help friends glue craft sticks into the shape of a star as shown below or make up your own patterns. (Glue guns work well for this.) Paint the stars with markers or highlighters and add tiny star stickers or glitter. If you wish, use a permanent marker to write a Christmas greeting or Bible verse on one stick. Attach a loop of narrow red or green ribbon to the stars and use them as ornaments or gifts.

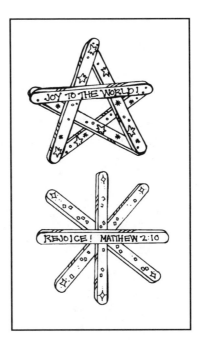

Materials

- Star pattern (photocopied from pattern on p. 149)
- Cardstock for star
- Aluminum pie plates
- Marker
- Scissors
- Paper punch
- Glitter, glue (optional)
- Cord or yarn

Directions

Ahead of time, copy the star pattern on page 149 on cardstock and cut it out. Cut off the rim of an aluminum foil pie plate.

Using the hand-over-hand technique, help your friend trace the star pattern on to the flat circle cut from the pie plate. Cut out the star and

punch a hole in the top. If you wish, run a line of glue all around the outside edge of the star and sprinkle with glitter. Tie a large loop of cord or yarn through the hole to make a hanger.

For a 3-dimensonal ornament, cut two stars from aluminum foil. Cut a slit on one from the top to halfway down the middle. On the second one, slit it from the bottom to halfway up as shown below. Then slide the two stars together.

LEADER TIP

Here's another idea for aluminum foil ornaments. Cut circles and other designs from aluminum foil pans. (See ornament patterns on pp. 137-140). Edges of the ornaments may be cut with pinking shears or scalloped-edged craft scissors. Help your friend as needed with the tracing and cutting.) Place the ornament on a cutting board or thick cardboard, and help your friend to use a nail or carpenter's punch to punch holes to make a design in the ornament. Punch a hole in the top, and tie with narrow red or green ribbon.

Materials
- Newspapers
- Plastic gloves
- Paint shirts
- Aluminum pie plates
- Red and green tempera paint
- 12" (30 cm) lengths of heavy cord
- Plastic forks
- Copy machine paper in various sizes and colors or freezer paper cut into various lengths

Directions
Cover your work area with newspapers and provide plastic gloves and paint shirts. Place a small amount of red tempera paint in a shallow pie plate. Use the hand-over-hand technique and a plastic fork to help your friend dip a length of cord into the paint. Swirl the string on a sheet of copy paper or freezer paper. Or place the string inside a folded sheet of paper; draw the string through to make designs. Allow the red paint to dry; repeat the process with green paint.

If string painting seems too difficult or messy, try sponge painting. Cut kitchen sponges into bells, stars, and trees, and so on. To make a handle, insert a large safety pin into each sponge; attach a spring-type clothespin as shown below.

LEADER TIP

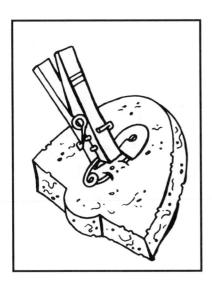

Materials

- Cardboard tubing
- Aluminum foil
- Silver tinsel garland
- Small Christmas balls
- Large needle
- Red or green yarn

Directions

Cut 1" (2.5 cm) sections of tubing from a paper towel tube or similar cardboard tubing. Cover with aluminum foil and tuck in the ends. Glue a length of silver tinsel garland around the circumference of the circle as shown below.

Thread red or green yarn through a large needle. Loop the yarn through the wire loop on a pretty Christmas ball; then stick the needle through the tubing, pulling the yarn through until the ball is about 1" (2.5 cm) from the top of the tubing. Knot the yarn to form a hanger. The finished ornament should look like this:

—Adapted from Trudy Vander Haar, *Advent: A Congregational Life/Intergenerational Experience.* © 1977, United Church Press.

Modeling Clay Crèche

Materials
- Modeling clay
- Markers
- Scraps of fabric or felt, glue
- Small box for stable
- Floral moss

Directions
Set out modeling clay and encourage your friends to make figures for a manger scene (Joseph, Mary, baby Jesus, and two shepherds). Allow the figures to dry completely. (Check at craft stores for various types of clay. Some can be air-dried; some can be baked.) Help your friend drape scraps of fabric around the figures and glue in place. Glue floral moss to the outside of a small box. Set the box on its side, and place the figures in the open stable.

LEADER TIP

If at all possible, have each friend make a complete crèche. If time or your friend's attention span doesn't allow this, have two or three friends work together to make a crèche that can be displayed in your room, used to tell the story, or given as a gift.

Materials

- Cardstock
- Balloons
- Scissors
- Markers or crayons
- Clear tape

Directions

Give each person a sheet of cardstock, and invite friends and mentors to draw things that remind them of Christmas. (Suggest things like bells, stars, angels, the baby in the manger, and so on.)

Curl the decorated sheet into a trumpet shape and tape the ends. Cut off the pointed tip at the open of the shofar as shown below. Cut off the tips of the balloons, and insert a balloon into each shofar, turning the "blow" end of the balloon inside out over the end of the shofar.

—Adapted from *Walk With Me*, K-1, Year 1, Unit 1, I Love and Obey God, © 2004, CRC Publications.

LEADER TIP

Explain that the shofar (show-far) was used in the temple to tell people it was time to worship God. The shofar was made from a ram's or goat's horn. When air was blown through the hollow horn, it made a trumpet sound. Sometimes the temple shofar was made with fancy silver or gold mouthpieces.

Use the horns along with rhythm instruments to accompany carol singing, especially if you use "A Christmas Psalm" (p. 42) as a praise and worship activity.

"Stained Glass" Nativity Scene

Materials

- Stained glass window pieces (photocopied from pattern on p. 147)
- Stained glass window frame (photocopied from pattern on p. 146)
- Star, Mary, Joseph, manger (photocopied from patterns on p. 149)
- Clear vinyl report covers
- Red, green, blue, orange, yellow vinyl report covers
- Black and brown construction paper, posterboard, or cardstock
- Dark blue or purple construction paper, posterboard, or cardstock
- Scissors
- Ziplock bags
- Lengths of narrow ribbon
- Glue
- Stapler (optional)
- Small suction cup hangers

LEADER TIP

This craft activity work best if the materials are prepared ahead of time and presented to each friend as a kit. Ask teenagers or senior members of your church family to help assemble the kits. Make a sample window so your friends and mentors can see the finished project, and use one kit to demonstrate the assembly process to the group.

Directions

Photocopy the patterns as listed above. First trace the rectangular-shaped window on the clear vinyl report cover. Cut the pattern apart, and trace the four stained glass window pieces on four different colored vinyl report covers (red, green, blue, orange) and the star on a yellow cover. Trace the stained glass window frame on black paper, the manger on brown, and the figures of Mary and Joseph on dark blue or purple construction paper,

LEADER TIP

For an opaque version of the stained glass nativity scene, use art foam instead of the vinyl covers. Follow the directions as above.

Or make a tissue paper collage. Copy the frame pattern on white cardstock; do not cut out the frame. Glue small squares of various colors of tissue paper to the window frame, keeping the collage inside the lines of the frame. Cut the figures from black construction paper and glue them on top.

posterboard, or cardstock. Cut out all the pieces and assemble them in a Ziplock bag, along with a length of narrow ribbon.

Give each friend a kit. Show your friends how to glue the four different colored pieces of the window to the clear vinyl by running a narrow strip of glue around the edge of the clear rectangle. (You may find it easier to staple the pieces to the clear vinyl.) Then, using the hand-over-hand technique as needed, help glue the black window frame in place over the colored pieces. Glue the yellow vinyl star off to the upper right of the black star in the center of the window. Glue the figures of Mary, Joseph, and the baby in the manger in place. Staple a ribbon hanger to the top of the window.

Show your friend how to press the suction cup hanger against a window. Hang the stained glass nativity scene on the hanger and watch how the light shines through it.

—Adapted from craft activity by Oriental Trading Company, Inc., P.O. Box 2308, Omaha, NE 68103-2308.

Materials

- Various Christmas stamps
- Inkpads
- Large sheets of construction paper
- White paper placemats (optional)

Directions

Borrow or purchase various Christmas stamps and inkpads. (Most craft departments and craft stores carry a wide selection.) Show your friends how to moisten the stamp on the inkpad and stamp the design on the construction paper. (If you prefer, use white placemats purchased from a party store.)

Placemats can be used for a Christmas party, or you and your friends could make them for Christmas dinner for a local nursing home. (See the service project section for other ideas.) **LEADER TIP**

Service Projects

- Caroling for Seniors
- Christmas Cards
- Christmas Cookie Gifts
- Christmas Letters
- Christmas Post Office
- Helper Gift Certificates
- Helping Hands
- Socks for Christmas

LEADER TIP

Some of the service ideas included here are old favorites of Friendship groups; others are new ideas you might want to try or adapt—perhaps your group could combine caroling and bringing cookies into one service project. Some of the activities in previous sections can also be used for service projects. For example, your group might want to present a drama at a nursing home or assisted living center. Or you could make Christmas decorations and purchase a tree for a homeless shelter. We've also included ways to turn service projects into fundraising projects.

Make sure everyone has at least one task to do in carrying out each project. Serving others is a wonderful way for your friends to discover and use their spiritual gifts.

Unless otherwise indicated, permission to photocopy material in this section for local Friendship program use is granted by CRC Publications.

Caroling for Seniors

Nursing home residents or seniors in assisted living centers will appreciate your group coming to carol. Plan a thirty-minute program of songs your group knows well (see pp. 99-121) and Christmas readings (see pp. 43-47). If your group is working on a drama, they could do a rehearsal performance for this audience. (You may want to use a sound system to be sure everyone can hear.) After the program, serve cookies your group has made (see service project idea on p. 85) or present individual gifts such as decorated placemats or ornaments for the residents to enjoy (see craft activities section, pp. 70, 72-74, 76, 81 and Christmas card idea on p. 84)

LEADER TIP

You'll want to start working early in the Christmas season if you plan to make homemade cookies and gifts. Depending on how often your group meets during December, you may find it easiest to plan an extra work session. Think through the transportation needs of your group too as you arrange to go away from your usual meeting place.

Materials

- ■ Cards (photocopied from pattern on p. 136)
- ■ Bright-colored cardstock for cards
- ■ Paper cutter for scissors
- ■ Old Christmas cards
- ■ Glue
- ■ Bits of ribbon, lace, beads, sequins, and so on
- ■ Paints, sponges (optional)
- ■ List of names and addresses or mailing labels
- ■ Envelopes, stamps
- ■ Narrow red or green ribbon

Directions

Ahead of time, photocopy the card pattern on bright-colored cardstock. Cut the cards apart with a paper cutter or scissors; fold in half to make a card.

Provide old greeting cards collected from your church family, glue, bits of lace, beads, and so on. Show your friends how to use these materials to decorate the front of the folded cards. (You may want to cut shapes from the old cards ahead of time. Or offer paints and sponges cut in the shape of bells, stars, and so on.)

Here are two suggestions for using the cards:

- ■ Bring a list of names and addresses of people in your church who are shut in, missionaries your church sponsors, children whose parents are in prison, children in foster care, and so on. Make sure you have at least one name for each person in your group. (If possible have at someone make mailing labels on the computer.) Have your friends sign their cards, and help address the envelopes. Stamp those that will be mailed or arrange for some of your group to deliver the cards in person.
- ■ Make a supply of cards for those in your church who are confined to their homes or nursing homes and are unable to shop for cards. Tie a bundle of cards together with narrow red or green ribbon and give them as gifts.

LEADER TIP
Making cards could become an ongoing fund-raising project for your group. Prepare a variety of patterns with different messages and Scripture verses for the inside of the card. Experiment with various kinds of paper, trims, and so on. Sell bundles of cards at a church bazaar or advertise them in your newsletter or church bulletin. Designate the money raised for a specific cause.

Materials

- Pre-measured ingredients for cookies, bowl, mixing spoon or electric mixer
- Prepared cookie dough or purchased cookie dough (optional)
- Pastry cloth (optional), rolling pin, cookie cutters or knife
- Cookie sheets, pot holders, spatula
- Latex-free gloves
- Candy sprinkles
- Frosting (optional)
- Serving plates, Ziplock bags, decorated coffee cans, ribbon, and so on

Directions

If you have access to a kitchen in the building where you meet, plan an evening to bake Christmas cookies. Depending on the space and the abilities of your group, either supply pre-measured ingredients for a favorite sugar cookie or gingerbread recipe or bring in prepared dough. (You may want to ask each friend's family or group home to supply a batch of chilled cookie dough.)

Have the dough and equipment set out as friends arrive. If possible, have several work stations set up for teams of about four people. (Make sure everyone wears gloves as they work.) Appoint one or two people to handle the baking. If you plan to frost the cookies rather than use sprinkles, set up a separate work station for this activity.

Make sure your friends are involved in serving and giving them away. Here are four suggestions:

- Arrange cookies on colorful paper Christmas plates. Slip each plate into a Ziplock bag and give the gifts to residents at the nursing home or assisted living center you visit (see "Caroling for Seniors," p. 83).
- Volunteer your group to serve cookies and punch after a Sunday morning service. Set up a serving table with Christmas napkins, punch cups, Christmas candles, and greens. If you made candleholders (p . 71) or an Advent wreath (p. 69), decorate the table with these. Arrange the cookies on large trays (you can do this ahead of time and freeze them).
- Serve the cookies for a family Christmas party. Set up a serving table much as you would for a Sunday morning. If your friends have younger siblings or nieces and nephews, your friends could tuck a gingerbread boy or girl in a sandwich bag, tie with red or green ribbon, and send one home with each child. (You might do this for children in your church nursery or Sunday school too.)
- Decorate coffee cans with Christmas wrap cut to fit or with adhesive shelf paper. Place a plastic bag in each can and carefully fill with cookies. Tie the bag shut, cover, and add a self-stick bow. Sell the cookies at a Christmas bazaar, or host a bake sale during mid-week

church activities. Designate the money for a specific cause—perhaps a family in your community who would not otherwise be able to buy gifts for their children.

LEADER TIP

In the welcoming activities section, we suggested making cookies to decorate a Christmas tree (see p. 35 for recipe and decorations). You could do this as a service project as well.

Materials

- Writing paper
- Pens, pencils, fine-tipped markers
- Sample letter on transparency or newsprint (optional)
- Drawing paper (optional)
- List of names and addresses or mailing labels
- Business envelopes
- Manila envelope (optional)
- Stamps

Directions

Pair friends and mentors or have small groups write letters to Friendship members that have moved away or to missionaries or others your group knows. Provide lined writing paper, pens, pencils, and fine-tipped markers. (It might be helpful to write a sample letter on transparency or newsprint. Or write sentence starters to help your friends highlight things to tell about your group and so on.) Encourage those who cannot write to color in a border or to draw pictures on the back of the letter or on blank sheets of paper.

Provide a list of names and addresses or mailing labels, envelopes, and stamps. (You may prefer to send all the letters in a large manila envelope to one person.)

Materials
- Folding table
- Large box
- Box or can with slit in lid
- Table(s)
- Masking tape
- Rubber bands
- Narrow red or green ribbon (optional)

LEADER TIP

You'll want to publicize this project in your church bulletin. Encourage members of your church to bring Christmas cards they plan to send to others in your church for your friends to distribute. (Decide if you wish to receive cards on one or more Sundays.) Ask church members to write the mailbox numbers or recipient's name in the upper right-hand corner (in place of the stamp) large enough to be read easily. Invite them to give a donation for a designated cause equal to the cost of the postage they've saved.

Directions
Set up a folding table in your church foyer. Provide a large box for collecting the cards and a box or can for collecting the donations.

Help friends sort the cards into bundles according to the mailbox numbers on the cards. Tie a rubber band around each bundle of cards (or use narrow red or green ribbon for a festive touch).

Have friends place the bundled cards in the corresponding mailbox.

LEADER TIP

Set up one or more tables along a wall in your meeting area. Write mailbox numbers on masking tape, and tape the numbers in order about a foot apart along one edge of the table.

If your congregation is large, you may want to presort the cards into four or more categories and assign teams to work on each category. Team one could sort cards numbered from 1 to 25, team two 26 to 50, and so on.

If your church is small and you don't have mailboxes, sort cards by last name. (You might ask senders to write the initial of the recipient's last name in the corner where the stamp would go.) Sort by initials from A-Z first, and then offer help to sort more specifically. Have your friends personally distribute the bundled cards to the recipients.

Materials

- Certificates and cover card (photocopied from pattern on pp. 142-143)
- Bright-colored cardstock for certificates and cover
- Paper cutter or scissors
- Fine-tipped markers
- Paper punch
- Narrow red or green ribbon
- Christmas stickers, wrapping paper (optional)

Directions

Provide each person with several helper gift certificates you've copied on bright-colored cardstock and cut to size. Encourage friends to think of ways they can help a special person in their lives (a parent, caregiver, pastor, and so on). Help them fill out the certificates either by writing or drawing a picture of the help they will give. Punch holes in the gift certificates and the cover card. Tie them together with the ribbon. Offer Christmas stickers and wrapping paper if you wish. Suggest that your friends put this gift in their special person's Christmas stocking, under their pillow on Christmas Eve, or by their plate at the Christmas dinner table.

Materials

- Poster heading (photocopied from pattern on p. 144)
- Glue sticks
- Light green or white posterboard (one or more sheets)
- Red or green cardstock
- Pencils, scissors
- Name/phone cards (photocopied from pattern on p. 145)
- Fine-tipped markers

LEADER TIP

This project provides a way for your friends to serve others in your church family. Each friend will volunteer one hour of service to the family who selects their hand from the poster you'll prepare as a group. You'll want to publicize this service in your church bulletin and do some behind-the-scenes work to make sure every friend is chosen, probably on one specific Sunday. (If you think your church family needs some convincing, pair friends and mentors as a volunteer team. Once families are introduced to your friends, you'll likely see relationships blossom.) Along with your team of mentors, be ready to assist with scheduling and transportation.

Directions

Ahead of time, photocopy the "Helping Hands" heading (enlarge the pattern on p. 144 if you are making a large poster). Glue the heading to a sheet of white or light green posterboard. (If your group is large, you may need more than one sheet of posterboard to hold all the hands.)

Have mentors trace around each friend's hand on red or green cardstock and help cut out the hands. (You will want to make the tracings slightly larger than the person's hand so the name/phone card will fit.) Provide a name/phone card for each friend, and help them write in their name, phone number, and the job they'd like to do for a family in your church. Glue the cards to the hands and glue the hands to the posterboard. Display the poster in a prominent place in your church.

LEADER TIP

You'll want to discuss this project ahead of time with your team of mentors. Mentors will know best what their friends can do well. Consider such tasks as baking cookies, washing dishes, playing with a preschooler, shoveling snow, dusting, folding towels, stuffing cards in envelopes, wrapping stocking gifts, decorating the tree, stringing lights and greens on a porch rail, washing vehicles, and so on.

Materials

■ Large Christmas stocking(s)

Directions

Early in the Advent season, hang up a large Christmas stocking in your room. (You may need more than one, depending on the size of your group and the response to this project.) Invite your group to bring pairs or packages of socks for children and adults at a homeless shelter in your community. Fill the large Christmas stocking(s) over the next few weeks, and arrange to deliver the socks to the shelter in time for Christmas.

LEADER TIP

If your friends need help purchasing socks, arrange a shopping trip or bring a shopping bag full of socks of all kinds that they can purchase at your meeting. You could use this same process to collect hats and mittens, school supplies, toiletries, and so on. You may wish to involve your entire faith community in this project, but let your group take the lead. (Consider other similar projects such as Samaritan's Purse, Angel Tree, and programs sponsored by your own denominational ministries.)

Materials
- Packaged snacks
- Juice boxes
- White paper lunch bags
- Markers, stickers
- Christmas stamps, ink pads (optional)

Directions
Purchase packaged snacks (granola bars, crackers and cheese, raisins, and so on) and juice boxes with a gift offering or money you've raised from a project. Invite your friends to decorate white paper lunch bags with markers and stickers (or stamp them with Christmas designs). Fill each bag with a snack and box of juice and deliver the treats to a children's choir during their rehearsal time.

—Diana Rock, Friendship Class, North Way Christian Community, Wexford, PA. Used by permission.

Celebration Ideas

■ Advent Secret Friends
■ Christmas Gift Exchange
■ Christmas Potluck
■ Epiphany Celebration

Materials

- Christmas wrap, square box and cover
- Index cards or scraps of bright-colored cardstock
- Photos of friends and mentors (optional)

Directions

Wrap a square box and the cover with Christmas wrapping paper. Write each friend's name on an index card or on scraps of bright-colored cardstock cut in various Christmas shapes. (If many of your friends cannot read, include photos of your friends and mentors on the cards along with the names.) Place the cards in the decorated box.

Set the stage by telling the group that the name they draw will be a secret. The person whose name they draw will become a special person for them to remember during the Advent season. They can pray for this person, do surprise favors for him or her, and think of special ways to make the Advent season joyful.

Think of a fun way to reveal the names of secret friends—make up riddles, have friends guess, and so on. Give a prize to the person the group thinks did the best job of keeping the secret. If you wish, have Advent secret friends bring a gift for their friend to your Christmas party. (See other gift exchange ideas on p. 95.)

Materials

- Name cards (optional—see directions for making name cards for "Advent Secret Friends," p. 94)
- Wrapping paper, recorded music, and so on (optional—see bulleted suggestions below)

Directions

Decide if you will draw for specific names or simply have each person bring a gift for someone of the same gender. (This eliminates problems if someone is absent the day of the gift exchange.) Decide too if you will include mentors in the drawing or limit it to friends only.

If you've drawn names, here are two ways to make the exchange even more fun:

- Write the names of favorite Christmas carols on notecards or scraps of Christmas wrap. (It's fine to have duplicate cards.) Have each person draw one card or slip of paper from a box or bag and sing the carol named before opening the gift. (You may want to help sing the first line and then have the group join in singing the first stanza.)
- Have your friends sit in a circle and pass around an unbreakable Christmas ornament while you play recorded Christmas carols. When the music stops, the person holding the ornament opens his or her gift.

Here are some ideas for exchanging gifts when you haven't drawn names:

- Ahead of time, make two sets of numbers on squares of green paper and two sets of numbers on squares of red paper. Tape the green numbers to the gifts brought by boys or men. Tape the red numbers to the gifts brought by girls or women. Place the other sets of numbers in two small boxes (one wrapped with green paper, one wrapped with red paper). Have each person draw a number and find the matching gift under the tree.
- As friends and mentors arrive, carefully rip off a small piece of wrapping paper from their gifts and place the pieces in bags designated for each gender. (In case more than one person has the same gift wrap, have a supply of stickers available to add a unique feature to both the gift and the piece torn off.) Have each person draw a piece of gift wrap and find the matching gift.
- Ahead of time, write a riddle or short poem about each person in your group. (Use green cards for boys/men and red cards for girls/women.) As friends bring their gifts, tape a card to each gift. When the group guesses who the person is, the recipient opens his or her gift.

Materials
■ Invitations (optional)
■ Table and room decorations
■ Tablecloth, napkins, plastic tableware, cups, plates (optional)

Directions
Plan a potluck meal as a separate event or along with a worship activity (see praise and worship section, pp. 36-52) or a performance (see drama section, pp. 53-65). Place an invitation in your church bulletin or newsletter several weeks in advance or have friends make invitations. Request that each family bring a salad or dessert and a hot dish. Provide bread and beverages.

Involve your friends in making table and room decorations (see welcome activities, pp. 30-35, and craft activities, pp. 66-81). You may want to purchase disposable tablecloths, plates, and cutlery to save cleanup time. Assign friends to help with table setting, welcoming, serving, and cleanup.

LEADER TIP

If many of your friends do not have family nearby, you may want to enlist the help of your church family to provide food. Suggest that families "adopt" a friend for the evening. Invite pastors, administrative and custodial staff, and others who have been supportive of your Friendship program throughout the year.

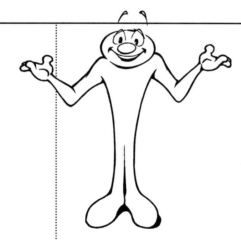

Consider saving the session about the wise men (session 2, pp. 19-29) for your first meeting in January. Combine the session with the gift collection and Epiphany party. Your friends might not be familiar with Epiphany. Here's a bit of background you can adapt to share with them:

- Epiphany is a one-day feast on January 6, following the traditional twelve days of Christmas. On the day of Epiphany we remember the coming of the wise men (or magi or kings) from the east. It's appropriate to remember this event apart from the Christmas celebration, since the Magi did not come to Bethlehem until nearly two years after Jesus' birth.

- Epiphany means showing or revealing. God revealed his love to the wise men when they followed the star that led them to Jesus, their Savior. These wise men were not part of the people of Israel. They were unfamiliar with the stories in the Bible. By revealing the news of Jesus' birth to strangers, we learn that God's love, revealed to us in the birth of Jesus, is not just for the people of Israel. It's for all of us.

- The liturgical colors for the day of Epiphany, as for Christmas, are white or gold (referring to Jesus). The main symbols are the star, which reminds us both of the star seen by the wise men and of Jesus, "the bright and Morning Star" (Revelation 22:16), and of light. The wise men were guided by the light of the star, and their journey to Jesus brought spiritual light into their lives. Jesus calls himself "the light of the world."

- This light also applies to God's people. Philippians 2 says we are to shine like stars or lights in a dark world. As we stand and walk in Jesus' light, we reflect that light so that others can find Jesus and escape the darkness in their lives.

—Excerpted from *Songs for LiFE,* Leader's Edition, © 1995, CRC Publications

Materials
- Boxes or bags for collecting used items
- Materials for stars and crowns (optional)
- Ingredients for cake or cupcakes, cherries
- Small prizes (pencils, pens, stamps, stickers, travel-size toiletries, and so on)

Directions
Make your Epiphany celebration a day of giving and rejoicing. Here are two suggestions for your celebration time.

- Gifts for Needy People

  Challenge your friends to act as the wise men, bringing quality used items in good condition for a shelter or mission project on Epiphany Sunday. Suggest that they bring clothing, games, books, cassettes, and so on. Provide large boxes or bags for collecting the items brought, and arrange for them to be delivered.

■ Welcome Back Party

If you've taken a break during December, a party is a fun way to begin the new year. You might make stars (see craft activities section, pp. 73-74) to decorate your room and crowns to wear (see pattern on p. 141). For refreshments, borrow from the French tradition of the *Gallette des Rois*, a cake baked with a coin inside. Instead of a single coin, tuck several cherries into the batter before baking. Those who find a cherry will receive a small surprise. (If your prefer, make cupcakes instead so that everyone gets a cherry to exchange for a prize. If members of your group have diabetes, serve sugar-free muffins instead.)

Songs

- Angels We Have Heard on High
- Away in a Manger
- Emmanuel, Emmanuel
- Gloria/Glory
- Good News
- Go, Tell It on the Mountain
- Hark! the Herald Angels Sing
- He Came Down
- Joy to the World
- Mary Had a Baby
- O Come, All Ye Faithful
- O Little Town of Bethlehem
- Ring the Bells
- Silent Night
- We Three Kings
- While Shepherds Watched

LEADER TIP

The songs we've included in this section are those we've suggested throughout this resource book.

If you have access to rhythm instruments (tambourines, sticks, maracas, and so on), add them to your praise and worship time. (We've included directions for making shofars on p. 78.) Invite a live band or instrumentalists to join your group, especially during the Christmas season.

To involve your friends who are nonverbal, we've added directions for signing and movement with several songs. You'll want to plan ahead how you will include your friends with limited mobility.

Look for opportunities for your friends to participate in worship services, perhaps by singing some of their favorite carols. We've also suggested caroling as a service project (see p. 83). Affirm your friends as they make music to the Lord.

 Unless your church already has a license to copy music that is copyrighted, you must request permission from the copyright holder to make photocopies, transparencies, or handouts of songs included in this section. Addresses are included with each song where this rule applies.

—Unless otherwise indicated signing directions are from Lottie L. Riekehof, *The Joy of Signing,* © 1978, Gospel Publishing House, 1445 Boonville Ave., Springfield, MO 65802. Used by permission.

For permission to photocopy signing directions for local Friendship program use, contact Gospel Publishing House.

Refrain

Glo - - - - ri - a

in ex - cel - sis De - o. Glo - -

- ri - a in ex - cel - sis De - o.

Words: French carol
Music: French melody

Words: American carol, 1885
Music: William J. Kirkpatrick, 1895

Emmanuel, Emmanuel

Em-man-u - el, Em-man-u - el, his name is called

Em-man-u - el. God with us, re-vealed in

us, his name is called Em-man-u - el.

Emmanuel
(Sign **God, With,**
and **Us,** which is the
translated meaning
from the Hebrew.)

God
Point the "G" hand
forward, draw it up
and back down,
opening the palm,
which is facing left.
Hand is raised
heavenward and then
down in a reverent
motion

With
Place the "A" hands
together, palm to
palm.

Us
The right "U" hand,
palm facing the body,
swings from right to
left shoulder, an
encompassing
gesture.

—Signing directions
from *Songs for LiFE,*
Leader's Edition, ©
1995, CRC Publications.

Glory
Clap the right hand against the left, lift the right and describe a large arc in front of you with the right hand, shaking the hand as it moves.

—Signing directions from Lottie L. Riekehof, *The Joy of Signing,* © 1978, Gospel Publishing House (1445 Boonville Ave., Springfield, MO 65802). Used by permission.

Spanish Glo - ria, glo - ria, glo - ria   en las al - tu - ras a Dios,
English Glo - ry, glo - ry, glo - ry,   glo - ry be to God on high,

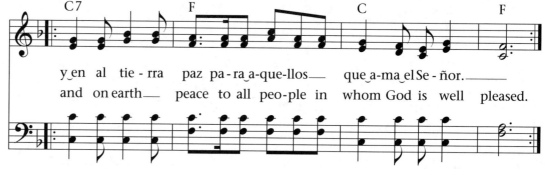

y en al tie - rra paz pa - ra a - que - llos___ que a - ma el Se - ñor.___
and on earth___ peace to all peo - ple in whom God is well pleased.

Words: Luke 2:14
Music: Pablo Sosa

Good News

1 Good news! Good news! News of great joy! For
2 Good news! Good news! Joy - ful - ly sing! For

un - to us in Beth - le - hem is born now a boy!
un - to us in Beth - le - hem is cra - dled a King!

3 Come, come, be of good cheer! Christ, our

Descant

News! News! Joy - ful - ly sing! For

Sav - ior, is here! 4 Good news! Good news! Wel - come the morn! For

Good
Touch the lips with the fingers of the right hand and then move the right hand forward placing it palm up in the palm of the left hand.

News
Place the "AND" hands at the forehead, move them down and away from you, ending with open palms up.

—Signing directions from Lottie L. Riekehof, *The Joy of Signing,* © 1978, Gospel Publishing House (1445 Boonville Ave., Springfield, MO 65802). Used by permission

Words and Music: Natalie Sleeth, adapted from the anthem "Good News"
© 1980, Hinshaw Music, Inc. (P.O. Box 470, Chapel Hill, NC 27514; 919-933-1691). Printed with permission.

Beth - le - hem's man - ger now cra - dles a King! For

un - to us in Beth - le - hem Lord Je - sus is born! For

there in a sta - ble Lord Je - sus, our Sav-ior, is born!

un-to us in Beth-le-hem Lord Je - sus is born!

Go, Tell It on the Mountain

Refrain

Go, tell it on the moun-tain, o-ver the hills and eve-ry-where;

go, tell it on the moun-tain that Je-sus Christ is born.

1 While shep-herds kept their watch - ing o'er
2 The shep-herds feared and trem - bled when
3 Down in a low - ly sta - ble the

si - lent flocks by night, be - hold, through-out the
lo! a - bove the earth rang out the an - gel
hum - ble Christ was born, and God sent us sal -

Repeat refrain

heav - ens there shone a ho - ly light.
cho - rus that hailed our Sav - ior's birth.
va - tion that bless - ed Christ-mas morn.

Go
Index fingers as they move forward, rotate around each other once. (When they give a command, the index fingers are swung down and forward, one behind the other.)

Tell
The index finger, pointing to the left, is held in front of the mouth and rolls forward in a circular movement.

—Signing directions from Lottie L. Riekehof, *The Joy of Signing,* © 1978, Gospel Publishing House (1445 Boonville Ave., Springfield, MO 65802). Used by permission.

Words and Music: African -American spiritual; arr. Emily R. Brink, 1991
Arr. © 1994, CRC Publications.

1 Hark! the her-ald an-gels sing, "Glo-ry to the new-born King;
2 Christ, by high-est heaven a-dored, Christ, the ev-er-last-ing Lord!
3 Hail the heaven-born Prince of Peace! Hail the Sun of Right-eous-ness!

peace on earth and mer-cy mild, God and sin-ners rec-on-ciled!"
Late in time be-hold him come, off-spring of the vir-gin's womb.
Light and life to all he brings, risen with heal-ing in his wings.

Joy-ful, all ye na-tions, rise; join the tri-umph of the skies;
Veiled in flesh the God-head see; hail the in-car-nate De-i-ty,
Mild, he lays his glo-ry by, born that we no more may die,

with the an-gel-ic hosts pro-claim, "Christ is born in Beth-le-hem!"
pleased as man with us to dwell, Je-sus, our Im-man-u-el.
born to raise the lost on earth, born to give them sec-ond birth.

Refrain

Hark! the her-ald an-gels sing, "Glo-ry to the new-born King!"

Words: Charles Wesley, 1707-1788
Music: Felix Mendelssohn, 1809-1849

He Came Down

He came down that we may have hope,*   he

came down that we may have hope,*   he came down that we may

have hope.*   Hal-le-lu-jah   for-ev-er-more.

(Why did Christ come?)

* peace, love, joy

Words: traditional
Music: from the Cameroons

—Signing directions from Lottie L. Riekehof, *The Joy of Signing,* © 1978, Gospel Publishing House (1445 Boonville Ave., Springfield, MO 65802). Used by permission.

Hope
Touch forehead with index finger; then raise open palms so they face each other, the right hand near right forehead and the left hand at left forehead. Both hands bend to a right angle and unbend simultaneously.

Peace
Right palm is placed on left palm then turned so left palm is on top; both hands palms down, move down and toward sides.

Love
"S" hands are crossed at wrist and pressed to heart.

Joy
Open hands pat chest several times with slight upward motion.

Words: Isaac Watts, 1674-1748
Music: George F. Handel, 1685-1759; arr. Lowell Mason.

Mary Had a Baby

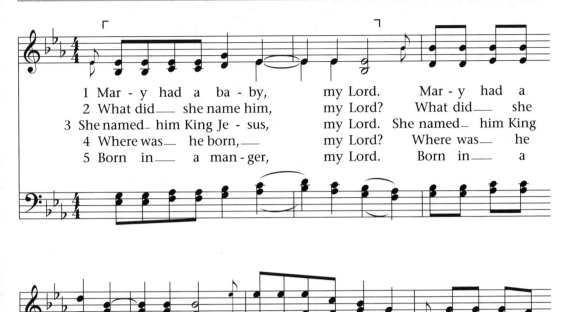

1 Mar-y had a ba-by, my Lord. Mar-y had a
2 What did___ she name him, my Lord? What did___ she
3 She named_ him King Je-sus, my Lord. She named_ him King
4 Where was___ he born,___ my Lord? Where was___ he
5 Born in___ a man-ger, my Lord. Born in___ a

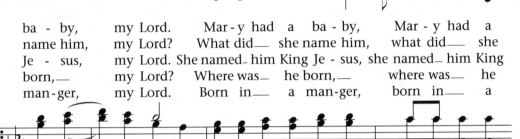

ba-by, my Lord. Mar-y had a ba-by, Mar-y had a
name him, my Lord? What did___ she name him, what did___ she
Je-sus, my Lord. She named_ him King Je-sus, she named_ him King
born,___ my Lord? Where was___ he born,___ where was___ he
man-ger, my Lord. Born in___ a man-ger, born in___ a

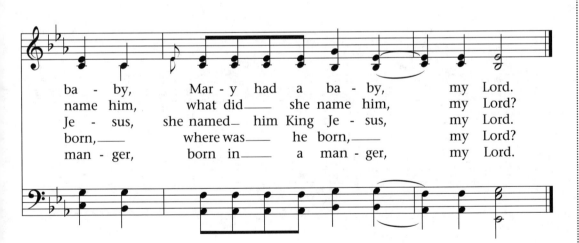

ba-by, Mar-y had a ba-by, my Lord.
name him, what did___ she name him, my Lord?
Je-sus, she named_ him King Je-sus, my Lord.
born,___ where was___ he born,___ my Lord?
man-ger, born in___ a man-ger, my Lord.

Baby
Place the right hand in the crook of the left arm and the left upturned hand under the right arm; then rock.

Lord
Place the right "L" at the left shoulder, then on the right waist.

King
Place the right "K" against the left shoulder, then against the right waist.

Jesus
Place the tip of the middle finger of the right open hand into the left palm and reverse.

Words and Music: African-American spiritual; arr. Kenneth L. Fenton
© Kenneth Fenton (10785 Valley View Road, #224, Eden Prairie, MN 55344). Used by permission.

—Signing directions from Lottie L. Riekehof, *The Joy of Signing,* © 1978, Gospel Publishing House (1445 Boonville Ave., Springfield, MO 65802). Used by permission.

1 O come, all ye faith-ful, joy-ful and tri-um-phant! O come
2 God of_ God,_ Light of Light e-ter-nal, lo,
3 Sing, choirs of an-gels, sing in ex-ul-ta-tion, sing,
4 Yea, Lord, we greet thee, born this hap-py morn-ing; Je-

ye, O come ye to Beth-le-hem! Come and be-hold him,
he ab-hors not the vir-gin's womb; Son of the Fa-ther, be-
all ye bright hosts of heaven a-bove: "Glo-ry to God, all
sus, to thee be all glo-ry given; Word of the Fath-er,

Refrain

born the King of an-gels; O come!
got-ten, not cre-at-ed; O come, let us a-dore him, O
glo-ry in the high-est!"
now in flesh ap-pear-ing;

come, let us a-dore him, O come, let us a-dore him, Christ the Lord!

Words: John F. Wade, 1711-1786; trans., Frederick Oakeley, 1802-1880
Music: Cantus Diversi, 1751

O Little Town of Bethlehem

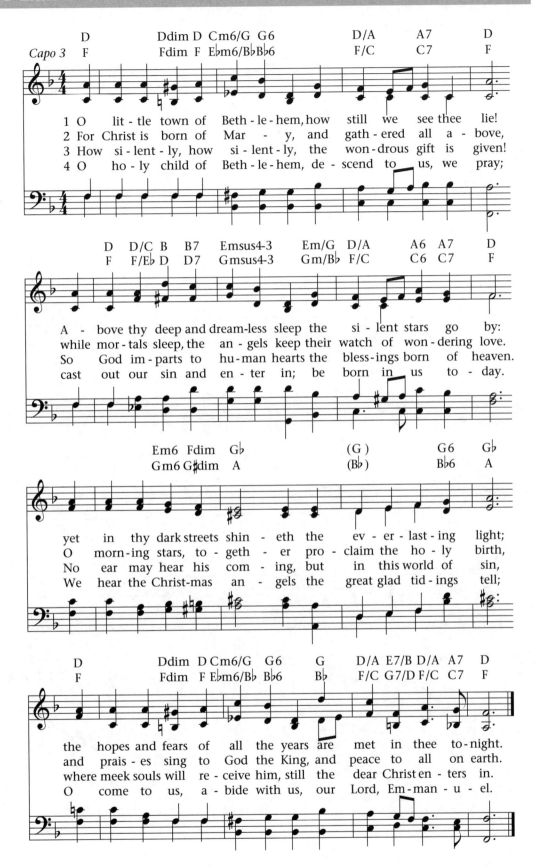

Words: Phillips Brooks, 1835-1893
Music: Lewis H. Redner, 1831-1908

Words and Music: Harry Bollback

God the Fa - ther gave his Son, gave his own be - lov-ed One

to this wick-ed sin-ful earth, to bring man-kind his love, new birth.

Ring the bells, ring the bells, let the whole world know

Christ the Sav - ior lives to-day as he did so long a - go.

Words: Joseph Mohr, 1792-1848
Music: Franz Gruber, 1787-1863

Silent Night: Dance Movements

Silent night! Holy night! (Start down low with arms down to the floor and head down. Slowly stand while bringing arms up overhead.)

All is calm . . . (Starting with arms up, bring them down in front of you, and sweep them out to the side, right arm to the right and left arm to the left.)

all is bright . . . (Reverse the above sweeping motion, ending with arms overhead.)

round yon virgin mother and child. (Make circles with both arms while lowering arms in front of the body. Arms end in a gesture as if cradling a baby.)

Holy infant so tender and mild, (Rock the "baby" to one side and then the other.)

sleep in heavenly peace; (Reach right arm across the body to the left side with palm up, and sweep it over to the right.)

sleep in heavenly peace. (Repeat with the left arm. End with both arms extended out to the side with palms up and head bowed.)

—Shelley Marinus. © 2002, CRC Publications.

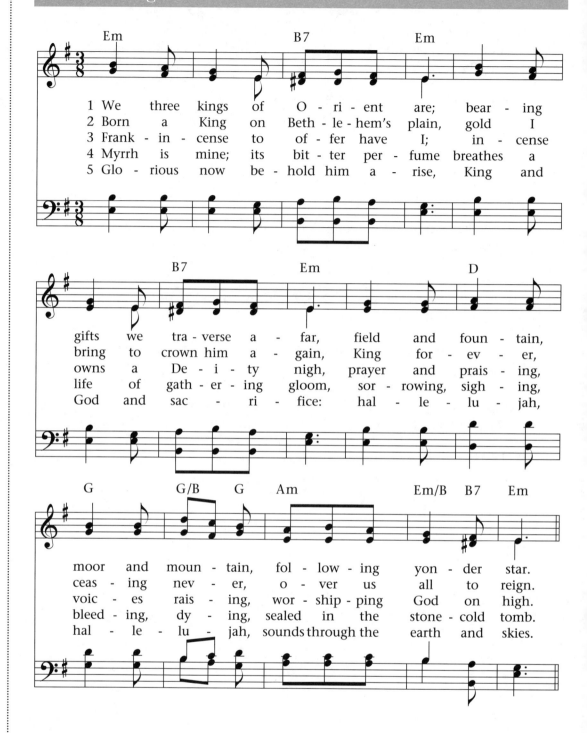

Words and Music: J. H. Hopkins, 1820-1891

Refrain

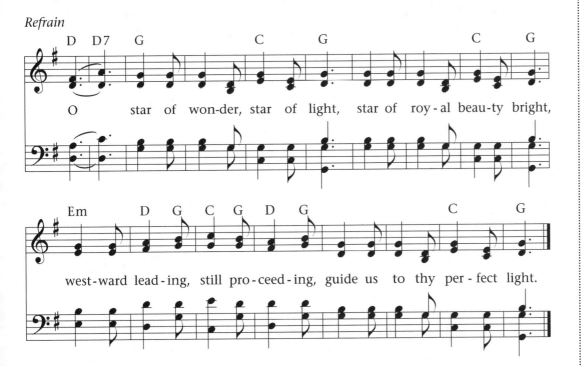

O star of won-der, star of light, star of roy-al beau-ty bright,

west-ward lead-ing, still pro-ceed-ing, guide us to thy per-fect light.

We three kings . . . *(Reach right arm out to the side, and bring hand up above head as if to make a crown with fingers extended up.)*

of orient are; *(Repeat above movements with left arm)*

bearing gifts we traverse afar, *(Reach both arms up overhead, and extend forward in front of body with palms up as if giving a gift.)*

field and fountain, *(Turn palms face down. Sweep both arms from side to side, right to left.)*

moor and mountain, *(With palms together, move arms up and over to the side in front of the body in the shape of a moutain.)*

following yonder star. *(Drop left arm to side. Bring right arm up in front of you on a diagonal as if pointing to a star. Look in the direction of the "star.")*

O . . . *(Bring right arm down to side.)*

star of wonder, star of light, *(Sway side to side.)*

star of royal beauty bright, *(While wiggling the fingers like a flickering light, cross arms low in front of body; then open up to a big circle above the head.)*

westward leading, still proceeding, *(Bring arms back down to side; walk four steps in the direction of the "star.")*

guide us to thy perfect light. *(Bend knees and bow head; then raise right arm on diagonal and point to the "star" while lifting head and looking at the "star.")*

—Shelley Marinus. © 2002, CRC Publications

1 While shep-herds watched their flocks by night, all scat - ed
2 "Fear not," said he– for might - y dread had seized their
3 "To you, in Da - vid's town, this day is born of
4 "The heaven - ly babe you there shall find to hu - man
5 "All glo - ry be to God on high, and to the

on the ground, an an - gel of the Lord came down,
trou - bled mind– "glad tid - ings of great joy I bring
Da - vid's line a Sav - ior, who is Christ the Lord;
view dis - played, all simp - ly wrapped in swadd - ling clothes
earth be peace; to those on whom his fav - or rests

and glo - ry shone a - round, and glo - ry shone a - round.
to you and all man - kind, to you and all man - kind.
and this shall be the sign, and this shall be the sign:
and in a man - ger laid, and in a man - ger laid."
good - will shall nev - er cease, good - will shall nev - er cease."

Words: Nahum Tate, 1652-1715
Music: George F. Handel, 1685-1759

Signing

■ Sessions 1 and 2: Memory Verse (Luke 2:11)
■ Session 2: Hope, Peace, Love, Joy

—Signing directions from Lottie L. Riekehof, *The Joy of Signing,* © 1978, Gospel Publishing House, 1445 Boonville Ave., Springfield, MO 65802. Used by permission.

 For permission to photocopy signing directions for local Friendship program use, contact Gospel Publishing House.

"Today in the town of David (Bethlehem) a Savior has been born to you. He is Christ the Lord."

—Luke 2:11

Today
Sign "THIS" and "DAY."

Town
Touch the tips of the open hands together as for "HOUSE" and repeat several times, moving to the right.

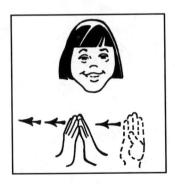

Bethlehem
Sign the "B" and "CITY".

Savior
Cross the wrists with the "S" hands, as if the wrists were bound; then bring the "S" hands out to the sides, turning them so they are facing forward. Add the "PERSON" ending.

Born
Place the back of the right open hand on the left palm: bring the hands up and forward.

You
Point the index finger out. For the plural, point the index finger out and move from left to right.

Christ
Place the right "C" at left shoulder and then at right waist.

Lord
Place the right "L" at the left shoulder, then on the right waist.

Use these signs along with the Christmas reading "So Many Gifts."

Hope
Touch the forehead with the index finger; then raise the open palms so they face each other, the right hand near the right forehead and the left hand at the left forehead. Both hands bend to a right angle and unbend simultaneously.

Love
The "S" hands are crossed at the wrist and pressed to the heart.

Joy
The open hands pat the chest several times with a slight upward motion.

Peace
Right palm is placed on left palm and then turned so the left palm is on top; both hands palms down, move down and toward the sides.

Patterns

Unless otherwise indicated, permission to photocopy patterns in this section for local Friendship program use is granted by CRC Publications.

You'll find patterns for story visuals for Session 1 and 2 and for activities described in steps 5 and 6 in the session plans. Other patterns will be used for various activities described in the welcome activities, dramas, craft activities, and service projects sections. Patterns are identified by the description used in the list of materials and by the session or section in which they are listed (see list on page 126).

LEADER TIP

1 2 3 4 5 6 7 8 9 10 11 12

13 14 15 16 17 18 19 20 21 22 23 24

Christmas Patterns

Thank God for Jesus!	Wise men saw a star.	Sing "Joy to the World!"	Shepherds came to worship.	Sing a song of praise!	Angels sang, "Glory to God!"	Sing "Away in a Manger."	Jesus is the Savior!	God sent his Son.	Mary had a baby!	Tell the story...	Jesus' birthday is coming.

Read Luke 2:1-20.	Wrap gifts for your family.	Pray for others.	Invite a friend to church.	Give to the home-less.	Bake cookies for a friend.	Sing Christmas carols.	Kiss someone you love.	Buy a special gift.	Help your neighbor.	Send a Christmas card.	Share God's love...

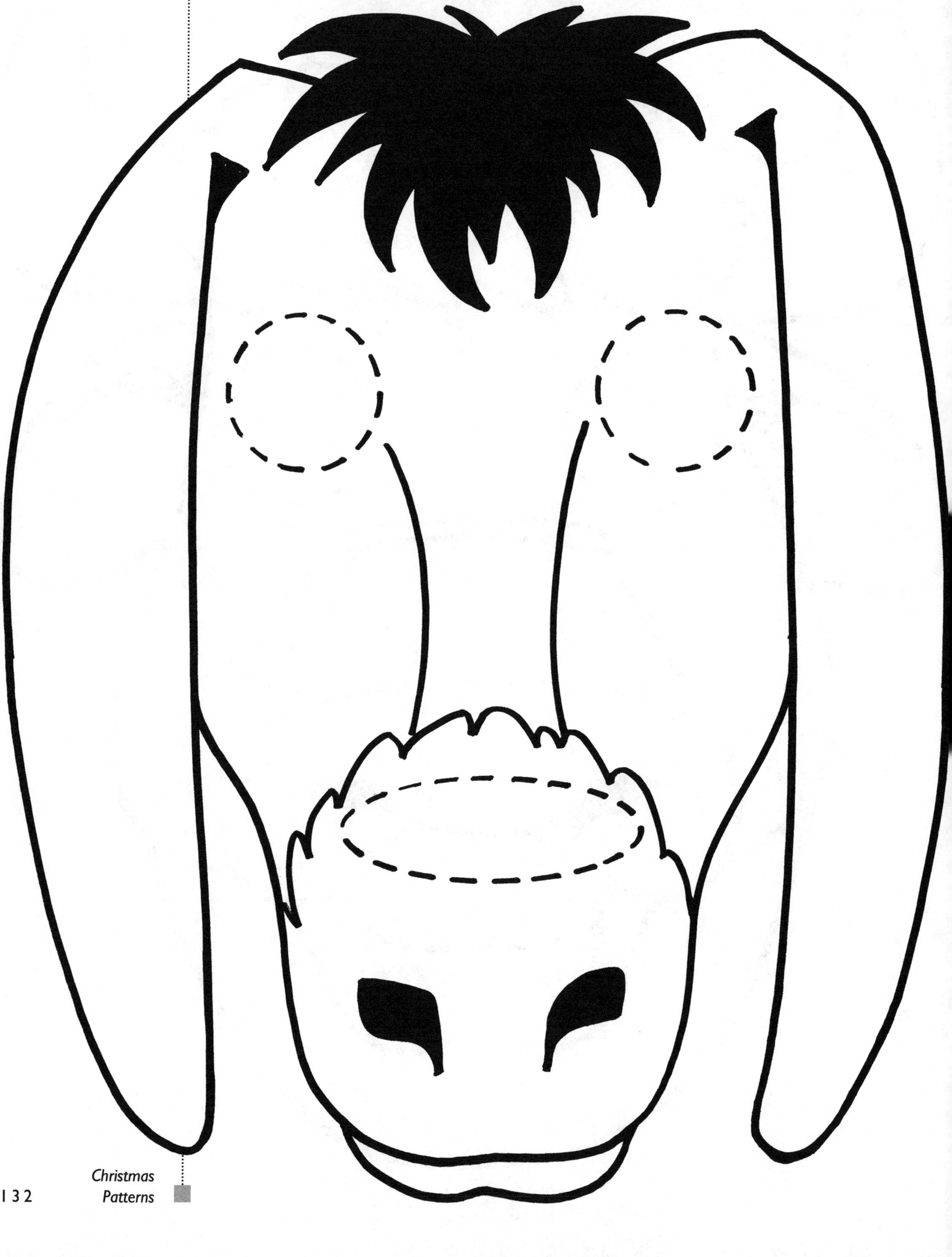

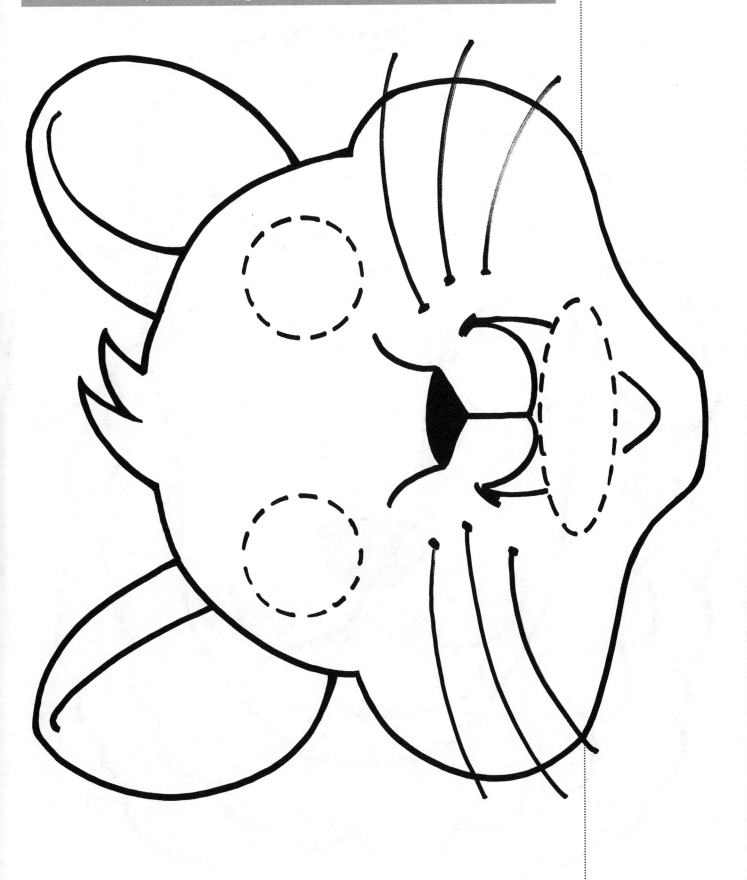

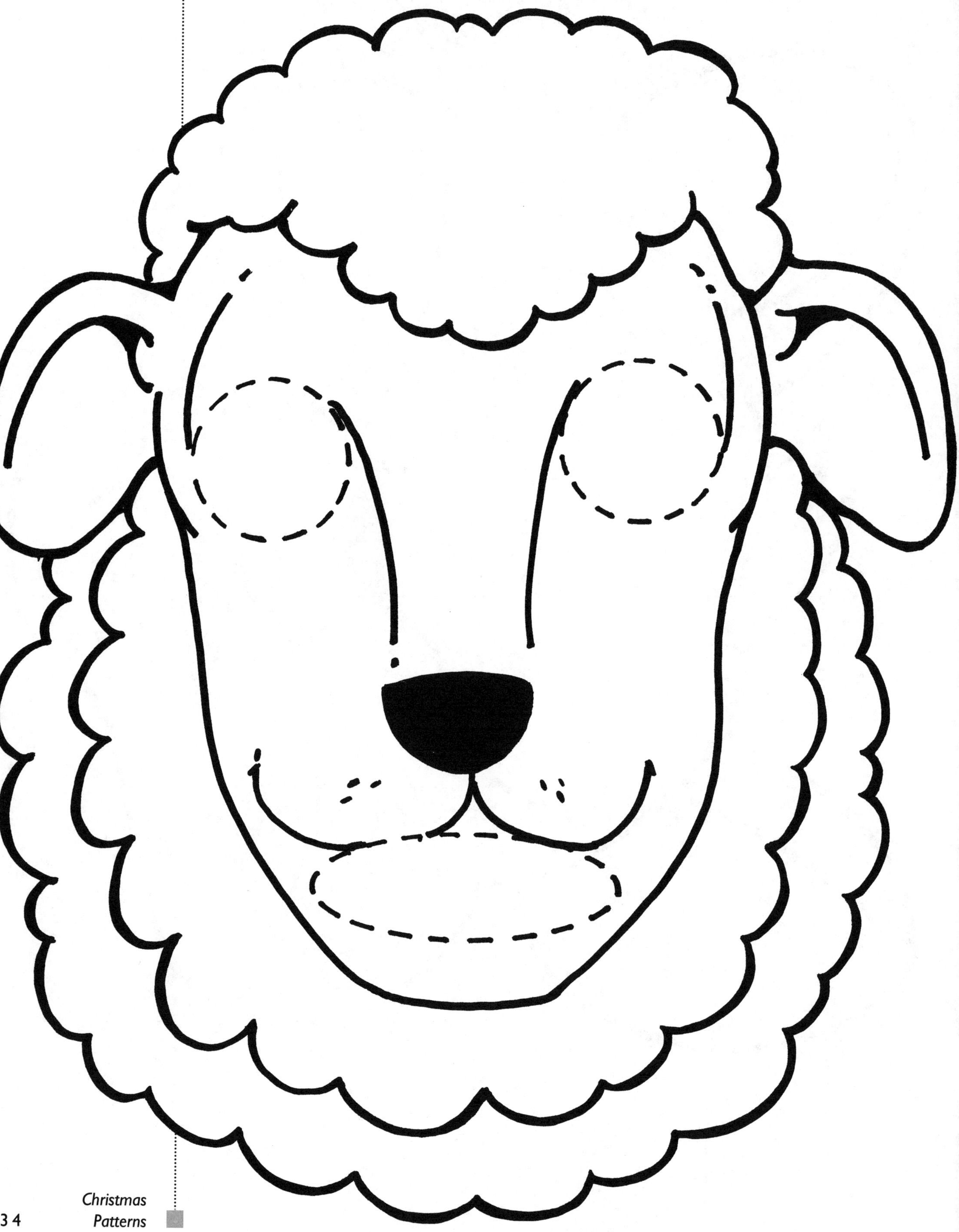

Wishing you

hope

peace

love

joy

this Christmas!

"Today in the town of David a Savior has been born to you. He is Christ the Lord."

—Luke 2:11, NIrV

Wishing you

hope

peace

love

joy

this Christmas!

"Today in the town of David a Savior has been born to you. He is Christ the Lord."

—Luke 2:11, NIrV

*Christmas
Patterns*

*Christmas
Patterns*

Helper Gift Certificates (Service Projects, p. 89)

Dear ______________________________

I want to be your helper. I will

____

____

____

(Name) ______________________________

Dear ______________________________

I want to be your helper. I will

____

____

____

(Name) ______________________________

For Someone Special

For Someone Special

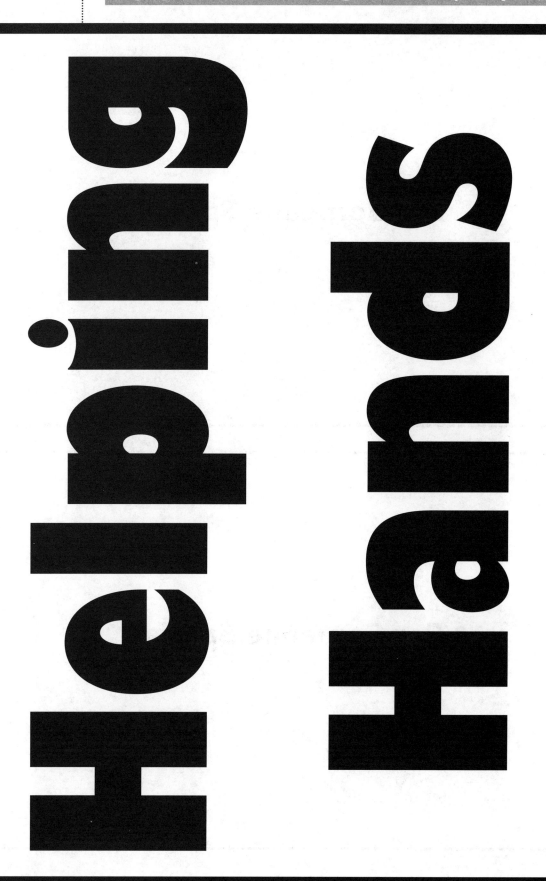

Name

Phone

I will help

Mentor's Name/Phone

Name

Phone

I will help

Mentor's Name/Phone

Name _____

Phone _____

I will help _____

_____

_____

_____

Mentor's Name/Phone _____

BLUE

ORANGE

YELLOW

RED

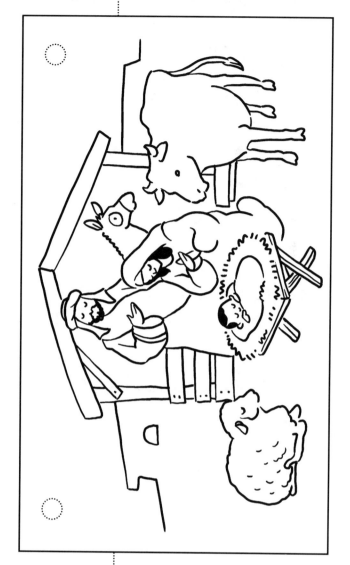

Christmas Patterns

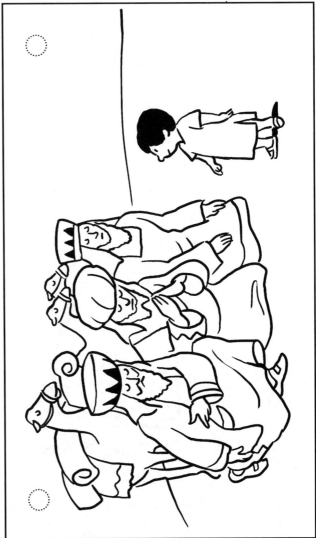

*Christmas
Patterns*

Christmas
Patterns

153

*Christmas
Patterns*

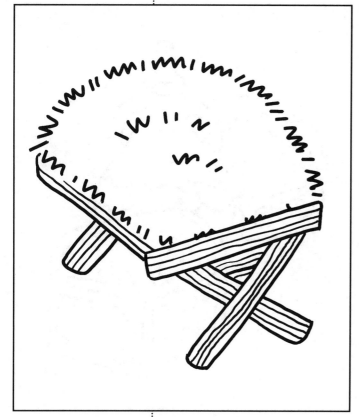

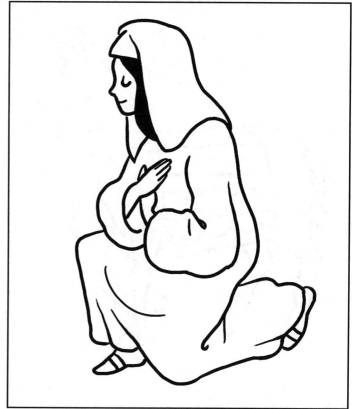

Evaluation
The Christmas Book

We invite you to take a few minutes to tell us how you used materials in this book with your Friendship group or one-on-one with your friend. Please complete this form and return to

Friendship Bible Studies
CRC Publications
2850 Kalamazoo Ave. SE
Grand Rapids, MI 49560

Or call or e-mail us at
1-800-333-8300
editors@faithaliveresources.org
friendship@Friendship.org

Things I found especially helpful or effective in this book were

Things I would change or add to this book include

Additional comments:

Name _____

I am a _____ group leader _____ mentor.

Church/Denomination _____

Church Address _____

Home Address _____

Church Phone _____ Home Phone _____

THE CHRISTMAS BOOK

Faith Alive Christian Resources published by CRC Publications.
© 2003, CRC Publications, 2850 Kalamazoo Ave. SE, Grand Rapids, MI 49560.

Friendship Bible Studies

God, Our Father (Old Testament)
Seven units tell the story of God's creation, God's covenant relationship with his people, and God's promise to send a Savior.

Unit 1: God Created the World
- God Made the World
- God Made People
- God Gave People Work
- God's World Was Spoiled

Unit 2: God Makes a Promise
- Noah (Building the Ark)
- Noah (The Flood)
- Abraham and Sarah
- Isaac and Rebekah

Unit 3: God Cares for His People
- Jacob (The Blessing from Isaac)
- Jacob (The Dream)
- Joseph and His Brothers
- Joseph in Egypt

Unit 4: God Helps His People
- Moses (The Burning Bush)
- Moses (The Exodus)
- Moses (Manna from Heaven)
- Moses (The Ten Commandments)

Unit 5: God Is Faithful
- Rahab and the Spies
- Joshua (The Jericho Walls)
- Ruth and Naomi
- Ruth and Boaz

Unit 6: God Works Through David
- David the Shepherd
- David and Goliath
- David Anointed as King
- David and Mephibosheth

Unit 7: God Gives People Hope
- Elijah (Fire from Heaven)
- Elisha (Oil for the Widow)
- Daniel (Friends in the Fiery Furnace)
- Daniel (Lions' Den)

Jesus, Our Savior (New Testament)
Six units are devoted to the stories about Jesus' life from his birth to his resurrection as told in the four gospels.

The Spirit, Our Helper (New Testament)
Six units highlight the work of the Holy Spirit in the early church as told in the book of Acts.

The Christmas Book
This resource book contains two session plans plus a collection of songs, dramas, ideas for worship, craft activities, patterns, and so on for the Advent season.

The Easter Book
This resource book includes two session plans plus a collection of songs, dramas, ideas for worship, craft activities, patterns, and so on for the season of Lent.

Index